There and back, a journey around my life

An autobiography of an owner driver

Chris Nicholls

D1335084

ISBN: 978-1-326-07010-6

ACKNOWLEDGEMENTS

I would like to thank my wonderful long suffering wife for allowing me to pursue my dreams. My surrogate brother Pete and his wife Gerry also deserve recognition for their support, encouragement and friendship over the past thirty odd years.

A big thank you goes out to all those men and women who have willingly or inadvertently wandered into my life. Their influence has made my challenging career interesting and given me wisdom with the strength to enjoy the wondrous world we live in.

FOREWORD

This book is a humorous account, an autobiography, of my twenty three year career as an owner driver between the mid-seventies and the nineties. It is a sequence of events with characters who have wandered into my life to make it a memorable adventure. It commenced when I found a derelict truck, complete with birds' nests, in a scrap yard and ended, under challenging circumstances compounded by VOSA. It includes a compilation of short stories, a written portrait of spilled secrets and recollections capturing moments in time. The latter were usually legal, sometimes dubious but on hind sight, often funny. The content consists of situations that should captivate and astound people, both in and out of the industry and much of it will ring bells of familiarity with 'old timers'.

CHAPTER ONE

In the beginning

For years I'd been told that I should put into print, all the tales I have repeated countless times to friends and, on the odd occasion, to complete strangers. These are the stories to enable my kids to understand and possibly forgive, the reason why I was often away at night or weekends unable to participate in fatherly duties on the sports field of their lives. Hopefully this book will explain why I have taken on any situation, often with unexpected or disastrous results in order to supply them with a stable home life.

Having driven in the region of three million miles in my working career, mainly without incident, a book could become very tedious after a couple of pages. Information such as 'Got up, drove to destination, unloaded and returned home' would not make for stimulating reading! Consequently, I have done my best to recall the experiences, people and places that have made my daily life memorable and also recorded feelings, whether good, bad or illegal which have made it noteworthy.

I'm in my local, beer to my right, which hopefully will provide me with inspiration. In front of me, sitting at an old table are three elderly gentlemen discussing the merits of motoring around the Scottish Isles. This is my moment to be begin.

Nothing stirred, the weather was grey and mournful, the type of day when you would expect a funeral to take place. It was 1976 and I had recently chosen to become an owner driver, a businessman or even an entrepreneur. This information I had recently broken to my wife over a meal in a quiet restaurant. She was not happy about my decision! The air that night was blue and she has not forgiven me to this day. I was bombarded with questions: "You don't have a licence or truck. Who's going to employ you? What do you know about

1

haulage? We have no telephone." My response was – "It'll get sorted."

At the time, I had a secure job being employed as a poorly paid photographer in an advertising agency. The prospect of a better standard of living, even to the point where I could pay for a family holiday, was restricted. My limited education, plus the disadvantage of dyslexia and chronic shyness, had prevented me from pursuing a professional career. As a country lad, being a vet had always appealed but in reality, if I wanted a better quality of life for myself and family, extra revenue had to be earned by other means! My dreams for the future depended on 'going it alone'. Without a penny in the bank an uphill course was about to be steered.

I paid for driving lessons in instalments over many months and on the third attempt passed my HGV class one. Why go for a class three when I could go straightto the top? A job as a tipper driver saw me do battle with the gear box of an S type Foden with a tipper trailer. A few months of this work confirmed my idea that haulage could be fun, challenging and rewarding. I was on my way to make my dreams come true and also in a position to answer a few of my wife's questions.

In 1978 a situation occurred that would enable me to become an owner driver, a wish I'd had for a while. One Saturday morning in November, while visiting my local car breaker, my dream truck appeared out of the mist. It came in the shape of a day cab Ford D800 unit and trailer entangled in a web of bushes and young trees. The wooden deck, piled high with old tyres and broken timber looked eerie in the greyness of the morning. This vehicle was home for many a feathered creature. Five nests were eventually removed from the chassis! The seats were originally black, but were now damp and mouldy with lack of use. White growth invaded the stitching. Tufts of moss sprouted like green beads along the windscreen. My dream machine stood before me but again I was skint. Where could I find the funds? A discussion in my local that evening provided the answer – obtain credit. The acceptance of the application form for the latter soon enabled me to be the proud owner of my first piece of plastic and may be this was the beginning of a financial slippery slope! With an agreed price of £125.00 for the whole rig being raised on an Access Card, I was now a businessman. Now all I had to do was rebuild the vehicle and put it to work. The idea of 18 hour days for six days a week seemed to be of little consequence to a young entrepreneur with his life in front of him.

It must be remembered, I was as green as grass. I could not tell the difference between a sausage and an arm pit! Reconstructing the truck occupied six months spare time. This took place, not in a work shop or even on a concrete pad, but on the ground in an abandoned orchard, tall with grass and overrun with brambles. On some winter mornings the dead growth from the previous year would be encrusted with pearls of ice, glistening in the low early light. In the spring, the creatures from under stones would visit me and leave their calling card in the way of bites. I was trained as a photographer. The only engineering skill I had at that point was the ability to rebuild a motor mower or tinker with old cars. I learnt by my mistakes and was given valuable advice from the owner of a truck braking yard. I talked myself into a short term job as a bus fitter to learn a little about heavy vehicles. This valuable knowledge also helped and eventually I secured an MOT for the truck. Today, I have the knowledge and experience to rebuild any commercial vehicle. I have never had a vehicle fail an M.O.T due to anything more serious than incorrectly adjusted brakes!!

I was now an owner driver on the way to my first million!!! This was a time when all you needed to be a haulier was a driving licence and a vehicle, period in history when CPC's, ADR certification, an operating base or statement of good character were not required. A log book was something you filled in at the end of the week, or in a layby if there was a possibility of the Boys in Blue having a purge. A flash of headlights and a thumb down from oncoming vehicle driver was often an indication of coppers lurking in the vicinity.

Experience has since taught me that the only way to make a million out of haulage is to start off with two! According to VOSA, the industry is not transport, but trans-sport, many participants but not many winners.

After a period of time all my wife's queries were answered and eventually after my persistent cold calling I was offered my first job. I had cycled miles around my home town, Southampton, leaving my details but without a phone number - instant contact with a potential customer was never on the books! At this particular place in the past, the GPO, as it was then called, had run out of telephone lines, mobile phones being only the product of science fiction, so it was many months before we were supplied with our own home line. In the mean-time our business calls were made from a local call box with its number on my business card! The latter was great for outgoing calls but poor for incoming communication and it must have seemed, to those trying to contact me that I was always out! No doubt, on the odd occasion when the receiver was lifted by a passing stranger, only a bizarre conversation would have transpired!

At last my totally re-built truck was ready for action. The first day of work arrived. It was seven in the morning and I was feeling buoyant. My vehicle ticked over contentedly. Lying ahead of me was an expanse of concrete building blocks. I was parked in the drying yard of a block making company with thousands of the lumps stretching towards the horizon like rows of grave stones.

"There you are lad," a voice came from behind the wall of concrete. The site manager had spoken and continued with, "Three loads a day is what our blokes do. Chuck' um on, chuck' um off."

A quick mental calculation produced a figure of 72 tons, the weight of an armoured tank or two.

"Do I get any help?" I remember muttering.

"Not from us you don't. You can bring a mate if you want. There might be someone to help when you tip."

I cannot recall seeing brick cranes in general use at that point in antiquity, if there were any, I could not afford one.

"The work's there if you want it lad. We will give you gloves to save your hands."The latter were great fully received. For some reason it had not occurred to me that hand- balling concrete blocks would rip my hands to shreds. The job was obviously tiring. Sleeping was never a problem and I ate for England. I became fit and lean. Who needs a gym? However the job itself became repetitive.

On most days my driving skills were never challenged but there were problems that lodged forever in the mind.

On one memorable occasion, the first of many over a twenty five year career, I had to drag a forty foot single axle trailer down a long, winding, single track lane without junctions or even field entrances. As I travelled down the lane, a terrible thought occurred," How would I turn?" A Chinook, complete with sky hook, would have been the perfect answer! I had anticipated problems and that is what I got. The house at the end, my destination and delivery point, had only a little parking space. Maybe on a good day there was enough room for three cars, but not enough space to turn my rig. I did not relish the idea of reversing the length of the two mile lane with the possibility of ruining a clutch in the process. An answer was formulated, tip the load, drop the trailer, go home and return with the solution..

The following morning was miserable. The rain seemed to hang in the air like a blanket. The answer I had devised had to be accomplished. With a ten ton jack I proceeded to lift the axle to the point where it became unstable. The rain fell relentlessly through the cracks in the trailer deck. It didn't matter where I positioned my head drops managed to find an eye or roll down my collar. Eventually, with a little persuasion, I was able to push the trailer over and off the jack. Slowly, inch by inch, I turned the trailer on its axis and eventually reconnected my motor. A day's work had been lost and I was cold, drenched but happy in the knowledge that a clutch had been saved.

Strangely, things always seemed to go wrong when it was cold, wet or dark. My God has a strange sense of humour. When the weather did happen to be hot, I would strip off to obtain a great tan on my six- pack. The down side of the high temperature was the dust, which stuck to my flesh like glue giving my skin the appearance of sand paper. I was entombed in a mixture of sweat and grime. The resultant mix itched horrendously. The only way to obtain some degree of relief was to stand against a tree or post and twizzle my body like a bull needing a good scratch against a gate post.

Following this three month stint of block delivering, having moved hundreds of tons of concrete and many pairs of gloves later, I found myself delivering to a high-gated, haulage yard. This was going to mark the first change of direction in my driving career.

Having, tipped the trailer, without any help from the builders, a lone body appeared. "I've been watching you drive. Hard work doesn't seem to bother you. Is this your truck?"

The chance of ending three months hard graft was irresistible. Three days later I had a new governor.

Most of the time, I was engaged in the delivery of French steel cladding, which had to be taken to all parts of the UK. Consequently it was not long before I had my first night out. In those days there were no sleeper cabs. You either put up with a door stretched across the cab with a li-lo and sleeping bag, or went into transport lodgings. Most bosses had a list of good accommodation for their drivers but unfortunately not mine.

My first experience of transport digs put me off forever. My day had ended in Birmingham and the idea of sleeping in the cab seemed daunting if not, illegal. The first establishment marked 'Transport Rooms' was approached as I was too tired to peruse the available stock of B&B's in the area. I was shown a tiny dark room decorated with green peeling paint. This was to be home for the night. A hole in the wall, courtesy of a kicked boot, the sole marks still imprinted in the damage, supplied a source of ventilation. After further investigation, a single bed covered with a flowery counterpane, revealed a couple of grimy stained sheets. I felt sick but the effort of trying to find other lodgings would be a struggle too far. Regrettably I chose to stay. God knows how many bodies had been there before me. Today, the smell of stale urine, reminds me of that room. I reluctantly lay on the top of the bed but in the morning I was peppered with bites, the results of hungry fleas. My day ahead was spent scratching the heads off the itching pustules. The only saving grace of that place was the king size breakfast and its incredible delicious smell. From that day on, until I purchased a truck with a sleeper cab, the door plus li-lo was the chosen crib.

As time passed I was considered for longer destinations.

"Chris", said 'Winco' owner and traffic controller looking up from his running sheet,"I've got a good little earner for you. Have you got a passport?"

I discovered later that this employer was a crap businessman but an honourable gentleman.

"How do you fancy a couple of days on La Continent?"

I had never driven abroad in a car never mind a truck.

"I dun know, I've never driven outside this country," I stuttered. I was shocked, talk about being thrown in at the deep end.

Winco replied, "It's easy, make sure you're not first off the ferry, then follow a local,"

I scoured my brain for a reason to duck out of the mission and stay in the UK.

"I've got no money or permits." This statement I could happily repeat today. I still don't have any money.

"I'll supply running money and sort the permits," he quickly replied.

D800 appearing out of the mist.

Sign written with a two inch brush and waiting to go.

CHAPTER TWO

To Switzerland

"I've got a trailer coming up from Poole in the morning with a motor-home to be taken to the Geneva Motor Show. Afterwards it's to pick up rolling frames and return home," my boss explained.

Caravan International in Poole, manufactured motor home bodies on steel frames which could be shunted around the factory, a push along production line. These were then loaded onto trailers and exported into Europe where they were fitted onto different vehicle chassis, Fiats, Renaults and Fords. Every now and again somebody had to drive around Europe collecting the now redundant rusty chassis and return them to Poole.

The stage was set, my forage into adventure was about to start. Oh shit!

For some reason I did not fancy the trip alone. Christine my wife could not come because of our young children but I'm sure we would have been divorced on our return if she had! I decided to phone a friend. Before I entered the world of haulage I worked as a commercial photographer in an advertising studio, the only thing I am qualified to do. The friend and surrogate brother, now of over 35yrs standing, worked as lay-out artist in the same studio. He was the gentleman who sign-painted my vehicle with the aid of masking tape and a two inch brush. He was about to make an instant decision for the first and last time in his life!

"Pete," I said, "Is your passport in date? Do you have any holiday due?" In what seemed like a couple of minutes, he replied, "Yes, why?"

"Do you fancy a trip to Switzerland?" I asked. Again I waited.

He repeated, "Why?"

"I'm taking my truck to the Geneva Motor Show, do you want to ride shot gun?" Pete's a bit of a car fanatic, very knowledgeable on many vehicles, but mostly VW's. Personally I consider these Marmite cars-you either love or hate them, a statement that puts me in the latter school of thought. The mention of The Geneva Motor Show was interpreted as, "I have a pair of free entry tickets."

"I'll ask the boss," he replied.

Things have changed. Today he would have to get permission from his wife, the real boss! Eventually a reply in the affirmative was given.

"I can have next week off."

Later, we met up as we do now, on Friday night at our local pub. Usually it is the time to put the world to rights, discuss problems and generally evaluate the previous week. This particular Friday was set aside for planning the journey ahead.

Which route were we to take? What accommodation would there be and most importantly what about our food? However the ferry was booked by 'Winco', so we had little choice of route. We were to travel overnight out of Portsmouth to St. Malo. One glance at my new map showed St. John and Basel, our point of entry into Switzerland, was quite a considerable drive. No doubt if I had a smaller map it would have seemed a shorter distance! Our route followed a straight line, where possible, passing through such iconic places as La Monde and Orleans.

.

We thought our hotel could be the motor-home until it was delivered. Cooking was to be done by Pete on its hob. After delivery we anticipated sleeping in small country hotels where classic continental cuisine would be the order of the day.

The following day, Saturday, was spent servicing the truck, checking the spare and hiding away our emergency rations, namely cans of Big Soup. The idea of breaking down never crossed my mind and spare parts and tools were not part of our itinerary. Sunday, the day of departure arrived eventually, but time seemed to drag. Waiting for the afternoon was a nightmare. I could not settle to do anything, starting one job then giving up just waiting for the minutes to pass took hours.

When, eventually the time arrived, I picked up Pete and collected my trailer loaded with a new motor-home, thankfully strapped securely in place. Our port of exit was Portsmouth, less than a one hour drive from home. Having passed through the freight office we positioned ourselves at the end of the truck queue and waited. The News of the World must have been read a few times before any movement was commenced.

After what seemed an eternity, the line of trucks crept forward into the bowels of the ferry where they were chained down. Ascending the stairs, we made our way to the lounge which was already full of drivers, some quietly reading, others supporting the bar and boisterously discussing the ways of the world. Being late January, holiday passengers were evident by their absence so the choice of chair or floor on which to sleep was endless. After a slow pint, tiredness crept up and slumber ensued.

I awoke, after a disturbed night's sleep on the floor, with a thumping head ache and stiff neck. A quick breakfast preceded going on deck to watch the sun rise over the silhouetted town. Daybreak felt cold. As I held the ship's railings the icy metal gripped my flesh to give a burning sensation. The freezing air engulfed me in its stillness. I have always loved arriving at new seaports and enjoyed seeing the workers go about their daily business. I find watching cities wake up more exciting than watching them going to sleep. Pete was probably still 'dead to the world' in his sleeping bag at that point and possibly snoring heavily somewhere under a table. A few years later he accompanied me to Germany on a business trip, his snoring then could be heard in the street outside our hotel. He has never been an early riser or a quiet sleeper!

Now back to the present moment. A cold shudder crept down my back. Before me lay, a calm sea as flat as my kitchen table. To my right was the beach on which a sole male walked his dog, he must have been an ex-pat, you don't see many Frenchmen walking their pets. The silhouetted port of St Malo began to show detail as the ferry approached the dock. Stevedores edged their way into position to take the ships' ropes. Within the space of a couple of minutes the Tannoy burst into life with the usual predicable recorded message, "Could all drivers please return to their vehicles?" There was no rush, no jostling as with tourists, most of these drivers were regulars who leisurely made their way down to collect their motors. Pete joined me in the stairwell, where the sweet smell of warm oil hung in the air. Together we made our way to my truck where we waited while the vehicle was unshackled. The bow doors opened to a welcome bright crisp French morning. Again we waited, and as advised we were not the first off. Following in a small convoy, we made our way out of the docks having been waved through customs. It was the first time in my life I'd been on French soil. William Tell eat your heart out, we were on our way!

St-Malo was a small town oozing with the smell of new bread that drifted into our cab. Little old ladies in head scarves and dark clothes seemed to be the only life form and all carried bags of baguettes. Chimney smoke from many houses meandered slowly skyward like twisting towers. The road ahead shone like a mirror. Overhanging branches glistened like bangles, the brightness of the morning light made me squint. An eight track tape was put on to accompany us on our journey.

Out of the town, long avenues of trees heaved with mistletoe. I made a mental note of a possible Christmas enterprise! Rusting Citroen vans, the ones that looked like corrugated iron sheds on wheels, festooned the drives of farms and country cottages. On hind sight a few of these old vehicles could have been a good investment! As the miles slipped by, my feet and legs grew colder, even the old rags plugging the holes by the foot pedals failed to prevent icy air from coming up through the floor.

Frequent stops were needed to restore circulation so a routine of jumping and stamping quickly renewed life to our toes. The endless miles of deserted roads dragged on for hours and we eventually arrived in St John as darkness settled. The border and its lorry park were easily found. This flat area of ground, the size of a football pitch, was covered in ash. It was nothing flashy with no hard standing, or security lights, just ash. In one corner was the customs control, a wooden shed reminiscent of a village hall. On opening the door, a cold dismal room greeted me. In front was a line of glass fronted hatches similar to an old English railway ticket office. The paint work must originally have been cream, now was discoloured by oily hands. On every spare inch of wall space telephone numbers and names were scrawled, vintage shabby chic! I picked a window and pushed my paperwork under the glass panel. This was grabbed, not courteously, but aggressively, somebody had had a bad day and I was the victim of his wrath.

"Non," was shouted at me, the paperwork then shoved back. I had heard customs could be difficult. I turned, to see standing behind me, two other drivers.

"Are you English I enquired?"

"Yer," one of them replied.

"I've never been through customs before could you help?"

"Fuck off," came the reply. I assumed this was a 'no'.

"Find a bloody agent," the other driver added.

At this point, these drivers cleared their paper work, left the building and blended into the night.

It was decided that the following morning was early enough to find the agent, food and sleep were a priority now.

The thought of hot soup and rolls tantalized my stomach, but first we had to enter the motor home. On trying the doors we found them locked. On looking through the driver's window, a key could be seen in the ignition.

"Now what?" I said.

Pete replied, "Keys come in pairs, the other one must be somewhere. Is it with your paperwork?"

I replied with, "It's not there"

"It's hidden somewhere," Pete retorted anxiously. He also was feeling the need for refreshment.

Eventually, after some meticulous searching, it was found taped to the inside of the bumper. Now for some food, but first, we had to light the hob. Within minutes it became apparent that this was a futile venture. The cupboard that should have housed the gas bottle was empty. Out went any idea of hot soup along with any thoughts of a warm vehicle.

Nourishment would have to be purchased and the nearest place was Switzerland. We escaped the truck park through a gap in the fence. A trailing dead blackberry bush was the closest thing to a border control barrier. Sustenance that night was the Swiss equivalent of a 'take away'. Beverage was taken in a bar before returning to a cold motor-home for a poor night's kip. Shivering in a sleeping bag to the grunting sound of Pete snoring was not a pleasant experience. God knows how his wife sleeps.

On studying the paper work the following morning, the name of the agent and our true destination became apparent. It was not Geneva but Zurich. Having completed our ablutions and having had a snack type breakfast in the take away establishment of the night before, we searched for the agent. Eventually his drab and inhospitable establishment was found.

The agent, on studying the papers was heard to utter, "Sacre bleu!" I assumed this was to pre-empt trouble.

"Problems?" I enquired.

"We," he replied. "How you say? Mickey Mouse permits, photocopies, you in big shit. Where is truck?"

"Over the border, near to the customs," I replied. The possibility of arrest and imprisonment suddenly appeared a reality!

"You go back, me come in an hour."

Sixty minutes passed and true to his word, the agent appeared and informed us that our vehicle was required in the customs shed. We duly unloaded the motor-home in the building and were told to leave the premises.

"You back tomorrow, midday."

Great, we were now marooned in a cold truck park, in a freezing cab, without our cargo and in fear of legal problems. From what Pete now informs me, we spent all that day and evening in a warm bar, drinking schnapps and befriending anyone who would talk to us. I do not remember returning to the truck but the next morning I awoke with cold limbs and a cracking head. To this day I don't know why we didn't book ourselves into a hotel.

At midday we returned to the customs shed, met the agent and reloaded the motor-home.

"I meet you at midnight, in lorry-park," he said. Again we waited, and again the cold gnawed at every extremity. The hours seemed like days, but about five to midnight the agent arrived carrying a small case. I assumed this was our paper work.

"You wait, me be back soon." He entered the customs control only to return after a couple of minutes. "You go now. Quick, very quick." I can only guess that something had been done, said or handed over to prevent a diplomatic incident!

We hastily left the vicinity and found the main road out of town heading towards Zurich. When the first suitable stopping place appeared we pulled over for yet another cold night's sleep.

In the morning Pete said he was getting worried that the week was moving on and he had to go back to work on the following Monday, today was Thursday. We had not even tipped our load and ahead of us was a drive back into France, through Luxemburg, Germany and Belgium. I also think a few more cold nights in a tin can, was not on his list of delights. It was decided to off load the motor-home and then head for Geneva Airport where Pete could catch a flight back to the UK.

The weather, on leaving Basel, was dry and cold, a few miles down the road we entered the Brugg tunnel. On exiting, we were met with a beautiful spectacle of thick snow, dribbling over roof edges like badly iced cakes. Fields unblemished by footprints glistened in the sunlight. The panorama was a chocolate box picture.

I dared not brake as the road was solid with ice and compressed snow. The back of my legs began to ache with tension. Although freezing outside, my hands started to sweat. I was also aware that a loo was desperately needed! By great providence a road side toilet appeared ahead. Oh relief! I slowly and carefully brought the vehicle to a halt, an ocean going oil tanker could have stopped quicker. I hastily jumped to the ground, my shoes sinking into the deep crisp snow before flying ass over tit.

Recovering my composure I tramped forward through the white stuff, sharp crunching, cracking sounds broke the silence. With my shoes stuffed with snow and overflowing with freezing ice I made my way to the toilet. On entering the small building, a graffiti sign was emblazoned on the wall and in tall black letters this aerosol statement greeted me 'UNITED FOR THE CUP'. A thought occurred to me, why isn't graffiti ever pink?

Zurich is big! We spent hours searching for the industrial estate without success. No doubt the regular drivers did not need a full delivery address, but a few extra clues for us would have been beneficial. Eventually we came to the banks of Lake Zurichsee, but were completely lost. It was time to ask for directions, a final resort I have always resented. The great thing about Swiss people is their ability to talk many European languages, so finding a native to give us advice was effortless. To our dismay our delivery point was a small town about 60 miles away but in the direction of Geneva! We retraced our journey before making new tracks to our destination and the car showroom.

A few hours later, I left Pete outside the airport to catch a plane home so the old dear would not be late for work on the following Monday! The rest of the day was spent driving back into France where I picked up steel from a number of premises. These frames were lighter than anticipated, but awkward to handle. Because of the nature of the product which was rusty bits of scrap, much of it had been left outside ready to be collected. When possible, I made my presence known to the owners before relieving them of their precious frames but sometimes if the establishments were closed I just took them, sod the consequences!

Saturday was spent collecting frames in Luxemburg. Nobody challenged me on entering this small country but trying to leave was to prove a little more difficult. Imagine a trailer half full of scrap, no paperwork to prove ownership or destination. It was night-time, I was cold and somewhat dirty. My eyes burned with tiredness, they felt sore as if grit was trapped under their lids. I was exhausted. All I wanted was a bath and home.

The German border was manned by a conscientious member of the Fatherland determined to follow his rule book. The diesel tank was dipped to determine whether any duty was due to the exchequer. It was difficult to explain to a German with limited English, why I wanted to enter Germany with an old lorry. With suspicion aroused I was requested to leave my vehicle and ushered into his small, intimate office where a fire burned furiously in a corner. The beautiful sight of embers spitting sparks into the room reminded me of our fire at home. Sitting at a table was an American airman in full uniform. He held a small glass of liquid refreshment. On the table lay a half empty bottle of schnapps. These two characters were obviously friends. The border officer explained his problem to the American. Why was this Englishman trying to enter Germany late on Saturday without paper work exceptfor a passport and vehicle insurance? Why the load of scrap he must have wondered? I explained to the airman my situation. He laughed in disbelief and after interpreting for his friend, further hysteria ensued. The customs officer unbelievably shook my hand and I assumed he wished me well! I entered Germany and parked up at the first available lay by.

I awoke on Sunday to find that six inches of snow had fallen during the night. Thinking back I do not understand why I hadn't frozen to death, the truck had no night heater or even a bed. I just curled up on the seat in a sleeping bag and put up with the cold nibbling at my extremities. The motion caused by shivering must have reverberated through the cab's body work. To this day I can sleep on top of a telegraph pole, but hate the cold.

I drove all that day, past fields of frozen vines though picturesque pine forests and past villages hanging on hill sides. The German village houses were square boxes, with pointed roofs all looking the same. The vast assortment of wall colours would put a paint sample card to shame! I drove to Cologne collecting more steel frames and finally drove back to Bonn, leaving Germany at Aarchen on the Belgium border.

As I crossed the country, I remember thinking how lazy German people seemed to be, as apart from army vehicles, I saw no other commercial vehicles that day. On approaching the border, an empty parking lane became visible just prior to the barrier. I pulled over and took my few documents to the border control.

"Why was I the only truck going through the border crossing?" I remember asking myself as I approached the building.

On entering the office I met Mr Hitler's brother, complete with moustache. I handed over my passport and insurances which was a trigger for all hell to let loose. Did he know something I was not aware of? Had England won the European Cup again?

"Yit is forbitten to drive zin Germany in Sunday."

This was news to me, something else I had not been told.

"Sorry," I replied apologetically.

He prattled on and on, his loud voice increasing in volume.

"If yit ever enter Germany again you be arrested."

"Sorry Adolf," I again replied, "I do not intend to."

True to my word, I have never returned to Germany with a truck since that day!

Having crossed over 'no-mans-land' into the Belgium control I again presented mypapers. One of the two duty customs officers came forward and stretched out his hand in a begging manner. I had heard of bribery and gifts being offered. Had these stories been true?

Would my entry into Belgium and my return home depend on a bribe? The other officer interrupted, and in broken English explained his fellow officer had been heavily drinking the night before and required small change for the coffee machine! With relief I handed over what little shrapnel I had left.

I resumed my drive into Belgium and onto Ostend. The two hour wait for the ferry was great, time for a wash, the need being rather urgent! If I turned around quickly I could smell myself coming the other way! A relaxing meal in the terminal was like nectar from the Gods. The sight of the white cliffs of Dover brought a tear to my eye. Back on the English roads, it took a couple of minutes to get used to driving on the left and I finally arrived back in Southampton, late on the Monday afternoon. If Pete had stayed the course he'd have saved an air fare and been six hours late for work!!

Another cold night ahead.

CHAPTER THREE

Stolen Propellers

I spent a few more months working for this company, learning new skills such as how to use dogs and chains. The art of sheeting and roping was explained to me by Ronny Shaw, a perfectionist when it came to a good looking, water proof load cover. This wiry driver lived for and loved trucks. His face, etched by the weather, gave the appearance of a man older than his years. His hands, scarred by accidents, could turn a straight rope into a secure knot, a dolly, in the blink of an eye. This skill, that takes most people many days to learn, is one that has never left me. I take great pride in showing off my ability to rope anything together, whatever its nature.

I remember accompanying Ronny into Ranks Flour Mill to load hundred weight (approx. 50kg) bags of flour onto a flatbed trailer. The bags would slide down a highly polished chute; the idea was to keep up with the loader at the top. The pace would increase the closer tea break approached. If one mistake, one slip or miss placed footing occurred, then an extra bag could and often would pin an unsuspecting driver to the floor. No such thing as health and safety in those days only laughter.

This particular day it was wet and very windy. The position of the mill, on the dock edge did little to help as a wind break. The bags had to be loaded, sheeted up and roped quickly to prevent water ruining the cargo. Unfortunately the wind caught the canvas sheets causing them to billow out like a spinnaker sail. My hands became red and raw and my nails felt close to parting company with my fingers. Gloves were not an option then, real men suffered rope burns and sore chaps. A large gust of wind finally saw me air born like Mary Poppins. Umpteen feet above the ground and holding on tightly to the sheet I heard Ronny shouting, "For God's sake stop fucking around." If it wasn't for the concrete breaking my fall, I might have hurt myself. In all, this was an initiation into how tough this part of transport could get.

Ronny was his 'own man', never understanding what the word 'can't' meant. It didn't matter whether it was looking down the barrel of a rifle whilst arguing with Spanish Basque Separatists wanting to use his truck as a road block, or shinning up a council lamp post to use the light socket to power his extension lead. Ronny took his truck home every night as he always had an early start. Nobody seemed to complain back then about noise or exhaust fumes. If a repair job was required, he would work late into the night, his extension lead and light being put to good use.

For me, the hardest part of transport was getting paid, my present company being no exception. Detaching money from its bank account was as easy as running theLondon Marathon. It was very exhausting, tiring and above all, it was a painful experience.

To ensure payment, Christine, my wife, would have to wait hours in the dirty outer office along with oily ropes and dirty sheets, often with our small children in tow. As is common with young children, the urge to explore the floor on knees was very enticing and many a time, the delayed receipt of a cheque was followed by a visit to the launderette!

If you were a subcontract owner-driver you would lose at least 10% of the job's value. This was the extra bit of money which went towards providing a good living or a new vehicle. The advantage of having an agent when working as a 'subby', was that you were fed work, however, if the agent went bust which was a frequent occurrence, the 'subby' could lose their money. Frustratingly these enterprises would often start trading again under another name!

Working for this company came to an abrupt end in mid-summer. On turning up for work one Monday morning, I found the gates locked. A small notice stated that the company had ceased trading! Looking through the bars, it was evident that there had been a clear-out. The yard was devoid of any objects relating to haulage, no trucks, no trailers or other transport artefacts littering the yard.

On the previous Friday I had been instructed by this company to pick up a heavily loaded trailer from the Old Docks, namely three enormous new bronze propellers. As I connected up, the afternoon sun reflected off each blade in shards of golden light and would have made an incredible painting. On entering the docks a few minutes earlier, I had noticed the weigh bridge was manned by ministry men. My stomach sunk, agents had the habit of falsifying load weights in order to 'legally' handle loads, an excepted practice and worked well until weighed. These officers were checking out the occasional trailer and doing their best to upset drivers and hauliers. It was my turn to play Russian Roulette. As I got close to the bridge I crossed my fingers and prayed. My luck had run out. I was pulled over and asked to put the whole rig onto the weigh bridge. It grossed out at just less than 28 tons.

"That's lucky," stated the bridge operator, passing me the weigh out ticket, "a few pounds more and you would have been over the top."

He had failed to check the details on the vehicle's plate. If he had, he would have noticed the maximum gross weight of this unit and loaded trailer was 24 ton. I was almost 4 tons over weight! My luck was in and I took my load a few miles back to the yard and dropped it. A week's work completed, off home for a well-earned bath and later, the Friday night visit to the pub.

Now it was Monday and I was horrified to be standing at a gate reading a noticewhich told me I was out of work! As I stood there, pondering my next move, a police man extracted himself from his panda car which was sheepishly parked away from general view, and approached me. "Morning drive, lovely day," he said as he got closer. He then proceeded to quiz me as to who I was and what I was doing. It was rather obvious I would have thought with my truck ticking over behind me! He took my name and address and informed me to expect to be interviewed in the near future but did not enlighten me as to the reason why!

It was a few days later that I was asked to informally attend an interview at my local police station. I assumed, if my cooperation was not forth coming, a summons would be! A convenient date and time was negotiated, but as I was looking after my young son, Jon, he also went along to the interview! We were welcomed at the station and cordially invited into the interview room. A long mahogany table run down its length and around it sat a team of plain clothes coppers. I was in for the third degree. They watched my every move. Although innocent of any crime, I felt guilty but pleased Jon was there to protect me from any possible heavy interview techniques. I had the only vacant seat so placed him on the table, his short legs dangling into my lap. I was informed that the trailer load of bronze propellers had been stolen over the weekend. They should have been delivered on the Saturday but had never arrived. According to the police and from the evidence from the weighbridge, I was the last legitimate person to handle this valuable load. Looking back, I must have been the number one suspect. As the interview continued, Jon became restless and noisy. Straining like a pup on a lead, it was not long before he became annoying. A young constable suggested a chocolate bar might appease him and the sergeant agreed. As this slowly melted his hands and lips became covered in brown goo. Jon failed to indicate that he wanted the toilet and it was not many minutes before a trail of wee slowly trickled and weaved the length of the table, steaming like the Amazon it eventually dropped off at a point between two officers. The interview continued, not one word was said by anyone about the tiny beck. Before I left the station I was informed that my boss had been arrested. He had run out of money to pay the drivers wages and stealing the propellers seemed the only way out.

CHAPTER FOUR

Rough time with a magistrate

My ego can outmanoeuvre common sense at times with the result that, unfortunately, stupidity sometimes wins. It was not long before the idea of a second truck crossed my mind! This momentary thought lingered and became a, "Why not?" If I could make some money driving my own vehicle, surely extra vehicles could only produce an extra income? This simple premise did not take into account the difficulty of finding a driver who matched my ability, enthusiasm and work ethic.

During the years that followed I used the services of a diverse range of drivers, from dim and dopy to highly intelligent; from honest to down-right rogues. In the late seventies and early eighties haulage was buzzing, the demand for vehicles being ferocious and this meant there was a demand for competent, reliable drivers. When I came to hire our first one, it was not long before I discovered the best were already employed. An advert in our local evening press resulted in only a single reply. I hoped this could be my dream driver, the beginning of a great trucking fleet, a dynasty with a related fortune! Christine and I agreed we should interview the applicant together. An appointment was duly made and we went to the applicant's house. This was for his convenience because at the time he was a house husband, a twentieth century new-man. This was a plausible profession according to my wife, but in the company of male friends I would have disagreed.

The house was a red brick council terrace, with a small front garden littered with abandoned children's toys. Twin tyre tracks were obvious on the poorly maintained lawn, indicating a vehicle had been recently present. The paint on the front door looked tired but if hung in the Tate Modern it would have won the Turner Prize. I knocked and we were cordially invited in by a short, well-groomed man. He introduced himself as Stewart. It was not long before he started to give us his hard luck story. Having been in prison but now released, he said he was determined to go straight if given a chance. He felt he owed it to his wife and family. On peering out of the window, we could see a back garden full of washing machines which he explained were scrap ready to be cashed in to provide extra money for his family!He reiterated the fact that nobody would give him a job because of his police record. Having done his time he wished to re-join the employed human race. Both Chris and I were taken in and decided to give him a chance. I checked his driving licences before offering him a job. He would use the Ford, the truck I had taken to Switzerland, as I was busy rebuilding an AEC.

Over the following weeks he was engaged on local jobs but all the time he was finding problems, forever phoning my wife complaining. He was mostly complaining about customers' premises. As if I could do anything about narrow gates etc. Where was his initiative? The day arrived when a load of fruit had to be delivered intoFaversham, Kent and then reloaded out of a London wholesale market before returning to the Southampton Fruit Market. Having loaded out of the docks and fuelled up, he departed east, on his way to his delivery point. A number of hours drifted past before he eventually phoned with his daily problem. This time he had hit gold and scored a bull's eye. Stewart had run out of fuel on the M2. The Old Bill had stopped to help. As is their way, they insisted on the usual walkabout, checking this and looking for any indiscretions which could lead to a fine and a few quid for the treasury. Having completed the vehicle inspection, with no detrimental results, it was time for Stewart's licence inspection. Jack pot! Stewart admitted he did not have a HGV licence. This information was passed to me by the police when informing me that my vehicle was about to be towed to a compound. They also warned me of probable prosecution for employing an unqualified driver! I never saw Stewart again. He vanished, only to speak to me over the phone explaining the incident. He was bright enough or too frightened not to collect his outstanding wages. This was good of him as it partly paid for the recovery of the vehicle!

I pondered for weeks about the mystery over the licence. I had, after all, seen it with my own eyes! I know I should have photocopied it at the interview, but how could I? At the time copiers were expensive, new technology which I couldn't afford. A few weeks passed before the buff envelope hit the door mat. An appointment had been arranged for my presence at Maidstone Magistrates Court. This was to be my first ever court case. I assumed, if I told the truth under oath all would be O.K. I was brought up to be honest. I felt confident in the British justice system. How miss- guided can an Englishman be!

The allotted day swiftly arrived. It's funny, when waiting for good things, time drags, only bad things come quickly. Dressed in my wedding suit and wished luck by my wife, I headed off in our old Volvo for Maidstone. The closer I got to the end of my journey, the sicker I felt. My stomach was very near the back of my throat. Once the court was found I parked up and made my way in. The clerk pointed me to the court room where, outside, I waited for my case to be heard. I sat down, stood up, paced about and tried reading the notices. I could not settle.

After what seemed like an eternity I was summoned. In front of me sat the magistrate and his entourage. An official read out the charge. I was asked," How do you plead?" I tried to explain my story but was interrupted with, "How do you plead?" I replied, "Guilty." The opportunity of stating my case went in an instant. Nerves, a tied tongue plus the lack of knowledge of court etiquette, put the kibosh on being able to speak up for myself. The word 'guilty' was ample excuse to finish the hearing. "You are fined £45 with three points on your licence." At this point, in a high pitched scream I replied "What!"

"Mr Nicholls, could you please pass your driving licence to the court official," responded the magistrate.
"It's at home," I replied.

"In that case you will be fined only. Please pay on the way out."

I have often wondered if I had left my wallet at my house, would I have escaped the fine. A court official duly ushered me quickly out of the court chamber and pointed in the direction of the cash desk, yet another tax collecting site! At this point nerves got the better of me and I had a desperate urge to find a bog. A notice on the wall indicated this small room was located under the court. Taking two steps at the time, in a desperate attempt to avoid an embarrassing accident, I soon found my way to the room. As I relaxed at the urinal I was joined by the very same magistrate who had relieved me of £45. I turned to him and in a mild, and now relaxed voice said," Good job that wasn't a hanging offence, or I'd be dead by now." His parting words to me were "Tough shit." Thus ended my high opinion of the British justice system. Over time I was informed Stewart, my ex-driver, had served his sentence for forgery. No doubt this included an HGV driving licence!

CHAPTER FIVE

My long suffering wife

If it were not for my long suffering wife and her support, I would not have been able to pursue my dream. She hated the dirt, grime and long hours away from home.

All my life, I have had dreams and wishes and have done my best to fulfil each one. From childhood I always wanted my own special girl, a friend, a lover, someone with whom I could share my problems, my thoughts and the good times. Christine and I met late in 1970 and within two hours I knew with whom I wished to spend the rest of my life. One year, one month, one week and a day later we were married. Having found her, I think I should tell her more often how much I appreciate her.

Number eight Portersbridge Street, Romsey was where our seedling marriage blossomed in a magical, grey slated cottage. Although it could be extremely cold in the winter, our first house was perfect. I can't remember a dull day, only bright ones. As the morning sun rose, shafts of light would penetrate the lacy curtains to dance on the dressing table and tumble to the floor. On Sundays, the Abbey bells would peel out across the town and meadows, worshippers hastily passing by our windows on their way to the service. In the evenings, the first to arrive home was Christine. As a teacher, the end of her day was earlier than mine. Having started the evening meal she would stand at the window and wait for my return. When I think back to those early innocent days, I can only smile.

All this came to an abrupt end when our land lady informed us that our contract was to be terminated as she wished to sell the property. The price she wanted was beyond our means but we did not want to find another rented place. We wished, as most couples do, to buy our own place. Romsey, even back in the seventies, was an expensive town. Our joint income was low. We were suffering the same problem that couples do today, no deposit, low income, pricey properties. Although there were cheap derelicts or rundown buildings available, they were for cash customers only. We were and still are a strong couple and had an unknown future ahead of us.

We have always worked for a common goal, in this case a house. We have the motto, we don't give up and we don't give in. Things would have to change; we would have to look outside our comfort zone.

We searched for our own first property and found a terraced house in Southampton, a twenty five per cent deposit was required but we had no savings. From where we stood, we could just about afford a 100% mortgage with a high interest rate. The latter was more preferable than trying to save a deposit whilst paying a very high rent. I say to young couples, we did not have it easy, we might have been the post war baby boom generation but the streets were not paved with gold. Admittedly there were jobs, a vast number and of great variety. It was possible for a young person to do anything or go anywhere. If you wanted to see the world, you could go to a port and find a job on a boat, this could be a trawler or an ocean going liner, all you needed was a passport and a little 'get up and go'. A job on a building site was down to brawn, not a certificate to drive a wheel barrow.

Our deposit was found, it was borrowed. We did it without help from our parents, paying the going rate. It was excessive, but we got our house, somewhere we could start a family. Money was always a rare commodity in our home but we did without. We had no furniture on the knock, just items bought from junk shops and auctions which we painted white. The closest we ever got to holidays was looking at adverts in travel magazines. Our car was so old; some fellow called Adam was the first owner! Pleasures had to be simple.

When Chris fell pregnant with our first child, Jon, money became even scarcer. As parents we agreed that we did not want our children to go to baby minders or to become latch key kids, an old fashioned home life was to be the order of the day. Chris was to be at home, looking after the family. We wanted the children's life to be a pleasure ground where stories and games meshed seamlessly into a natural world free of consumer pressures. As the bread-winner, my role was to enable these things to be possible, often grafting all the hours God created. Being at home was not an excuse for Chris to sleep in. Each morning, no matter how early, she cooked me a breakfast. Spoilt or what? Breakfast, up the road, would be the full English, often affectionately called the full Monty, 'eighteen wheeler', or even' the gut buster'. I have always believed a hearty breakfast sets one up for the day, hunger makes me awfully niggled and short tempered!

In order to produce extra funds for the family coffers, we took in students. On one occasion four, fresh faced boys just out of nappies came to live with us. This group of university 'fresher's' contained a rather posh lad, a very 'yar yar' gentleman, complete with his own private booze cabinet supplied by daddy. One of his roommates, a mild student, was encouraged on one particular evening to' grow up' and participate in the joys of whisky. Christine remembers slipping down the stairs after this lad had thrown up during the night!

We had many bodies over the years, clogging up the bathroom. They included home sick mature students waiting for Friday nights and an Irish navvy who would spend longer bathing and scrubbing than any woman. Chris thought this man was a secret IRA bomber! The other extreme was a very pretty, large girl, who would never wash. Her sound knowledge of fashion could change her instantly from a dirty scruff into a creature of beauty with just the addition of a scarf or a few accessories. She thought nothing of shovelling a whole cheese cake into herself at one sitting!

Numerous 'make a million ideas' made brief appearances over the years, the manufacture of four poster beds was one of the first. This enterprise attracted enquires from America and Australia after we placed an advert in Country Life. Lack of funds brought this, potentially great scheme, to a rapid close. Exporting car parts, although attracting a lot of international inquires following the sending off of leaflets, suffered the same financial fate. Many years later the exporting of household spares to Oman was successful but died a death with the invasion of Kuwait.

Special family time was scarce as I was away so much. Contact was made by phone every evening, assuming I could find a box that hadn't been vandalized! Mobile phones had not arrived. Weekends were no better, as I had to spend time servicing or repairing motors. The more trucks I owned, the more time I spent away from the family. My wife got comfort, advice and friendship from our near neighbours. A number of these have remained close friends to the present day. We watched their children grow up, struggle with the pains of adolescence and marry. In the house opposite was Teresa, a Northern Lass, married to an Irish milkman. She, a proud committed Catholic, produced countless children until the novelty wore off! Little Chrissy, a grandmother figure, acted as a substitute 'mum' when my wife had a down moment. Miss Prim, Jenny, and her mother lived at number 11. Mum was a member of a past generation of ladies who attended weekly sewing circles. Then there was' Mad Mary', she rode everywhere on her bike nicking toilet rolls! Sue and Dave, with their daughter Sarah, occupied the house next door. Moira and her husband, both teachers with daughter Kirsty plus siblings owned house number 9. Kirsty was my daughter Beth's best friend, their rivalry in every academic subject helped to encourage both to achieve great results in their "O" levels. Shruti and her husband Aftab came from Kenya and with their two children occupied no 15 which was diagonally to the right of our home while wonderful Mrs. Harbut lived diagonally to the left. She was so old that she must have been receiving the queen's birthday telegram for years. On Sundays Teresa supplied and delivered lunch to her. One Christmas Eve our children left mince-pies on the door step then pressed the door bell and scarpered home. We watched, through our curtains, to see her discover a gift from Santa! Every week the young mothers took it in turns to host a Tuesday meeting. This was a welcome break for Chris, unless it was her turn to clean up the aftermath of lots of children's toys and food!

Livingstone Rd had a community spirit that is not often replicated these days.

CHAPTER SIX

Stolen apples

With the demise of Stewart, the need for a replacement driver became imperative. A small advertisement in our evening news paper resulted in the appointment of Mike Irons, a faithful driver and friend for over eight years. Mike's previous employer was H M Government, as a driver in the Army. This job terminated when an IRA sniper put a perfectly round hole in his regimental beret! His wife, at that point, gave him an ultimatum," Leave the Army or I'll leave you." She was a girl with a spectacular figure so it was no contest. Mike had little choice but to enter Civvy Street!

I learnt, over the years, nothing worried him; he was insensitive to danger. On one occasion, whilst driving for the SAS in Aden, he took cover under the fuel tanker he was driving when the enemy thought it would be a laugh to use him for target practice. This, as a place of safety must be at the bottom of my list! His idea of reckless driving was to put any passenger to sleep with his uneventful, calm skills. This laid back manner first manifested itself when taking his HGV driving test. As a young recruit in the army, he trained to be a driver. Seemingly, on one particular, very warm sunny day, after many hours of training, he was walking across the parade ground when the driving examiner approached him. "Irons!"

"Yes sir," Mike replied.

"Have you taken your test yet?"

"No sir."

At which point the examiner pointed to a truck, "We'll do it now in that vehicle."

"Yes sir."

Within a few minutes of starting the test drive, the examiner, drenched in warm sun, fell asleep. It was after a few hours of driving around the county that he awoke.

"Have I been asleep long Irons?"

"Yes sir, about two hours, sir."

The examiner stated he must be a good driver and issued a pass certificate!

When Mike started working for me, I was still utilising the orchard for the servicing of vehicles. On occasions when it was necessary to venture under a vehicle, used fertilizer bags were placed on the ground. In winter they were used in the vain hope of that they would keep out the cold and damp whilst in summer used as a barrier against insects. No wonder I have a bad back and a hatred of bugs to this day! The workshop was a 'high tech', wooden chicken house. The word, 'high- tech' meant, it was dry. The closest thing to a radio was the sweet chorus of bird song, not a bad sound on a fresh sunny morning in spring when morning mists hugged the valleys before the sun burnt them off. There was no electric or running water, no chance of a lingering brew. The plus side of the orchard was the nearby pub that acted as a canteen at the end of a working day. I am surprised that the Landlord allowed us into the building as we were often covered from head to foot in oil and dirt. For an unknown reason oil has always migrated to my face to make me look like the traditional Welsh coal miner. In time this amateurish work space was superseded by a pigsty in the grounds of an old coal yard in Southampton. I must point out that the pigsty was in due course modified, stretched, pulled and enlarged by myself and Mike

It became a professional work shop capable of holding one truck undercover and provided proper facilities for everyday maintenance and MOT preparation. The general untidiness of the building still was reminiscent of a pigsty. Has anything really changed in my workshop conditions?

My transport fleet comprised, at this point, of two AEC's. The second truck I purchased from a breaker's yard for the glorious sum of £500. The original owner, the founder of one of the South's largest plant hire companies, was going through a cash flow crisis. His one and only daughter had decided to get married in a hurry I assume father was holding a shot gun, and the sale of the truck paid for the wedding! When, I eventually sold it, two and a half years later, I collected £450, not bad depreciation.

Up until the early nineties refrigerated cargo ships from South Africa, regularly off loaded perishable fruit into Southampton for delivery to wholesale markets throughout the country. I remember apples, pears and grapes were the most common with oranges coming from the Mediterranean region. Every year, it was rumoured that a complete ship load of fruit, arriving from South Africa, would 'go walkies' by the end of the season. Seemingly the authorities were clueless as to how a ship of fruit could disappear. Obviously, with the introduction of containers plus computer tracking, the monitoring and control of fruit movements became a more accurate science. As far as I am aware, no driver I employed was in on the scam, but I understand many were according to drivers' stories. There again, they have great imaginations and it does not take long for a story to become the gospel truth, commercial 'Chinese Whispers'.

Cars and holidays were said to be the usual rewards for the risk. Grapes topped the list of goodies stolen as they offered the best returns. Forty foot trailers provided the perfect platform to remove cargo. The bed of the trailer took twenty pallets if loaded one way but if they were turned through ninety degrees, twenty two could be stowed. The idea, so I have been informed, was to pace the loading of your trailer to coincide with the considerable breaks taken by the dockies. When twenty pallets, the designed full load, had been forklifted on to a trailer, a checker would sign the dock pass, your 'get out of jail card.' Promptly, at the designated time, the checker would hastily depart the scene to enjoy yet another cup of tea, steaming pies and a fag. This was the signal to the odd rogue fork truck driver, often the last man in for a tea break, to slip a couple of extra pallets onto the rear end of any trailer in return for a contribution from the driver towards his holiday fund. The lorry driver could now sheet and tie his load complete with two extra pallets. Today the loading of such vehicles would be watched by CTV and overseen by an outside security company.

The truck and load, trussed up like a chicken, would exit the dock after handing over the pass to the duty police officer on the gate to enter 'Freedom'. The loads were never checked, well not the ones I handled. If the destination was a London market, the vehicle and trailer would be parked on any area of waste land or back street until nightfall. Loads of fruit rarely got plundered by opportunists as no-one argued with a burly driver who was capable of a thump powerful enough to put Santa into orbit!

Come late evening, as the most sensible of members of the community had settled down in front of the television, the vehicles would set off for the Smoke.

In the markets there were, according to drivers' stories, a number of unscrupulous traders who would happily purchase any extra pallets of fruit. It was rumoured that one owner driver was owed so much cash from his deals, that a sack was required at the end of the season to cart his gains home!

Obviously the dock police, in their wisdom, wanted to make an example of any driver caught pilfering, a deterrent to stop the wholesale theft of fruit. In their dreams! A good criminal is always one step ahead of the Old Bill. My driver, Mike Irons was one of their victims when he was accused of pilfering. One lunch time, when I was in my workshop, I received a phone call from the docks' police. They had apprehended him for stealing apples and wished me to press charges against. They had picked the wrong bloke. Mike was rather old fashioned and believed in the same values as me including honesty and honesty at all times, even if people got hurt with the truth. So it was, with a certain amount of curiosity, I rushed to the docks to defend my man. Two dock coppers greeted me and took it in turns to explain Mike's dreadful deed. From their office, a view point overlooking the quay, they had watched him inspect the security of his load. He was a true professional, ropes had to be tight and every load looked like a carefully wrapped parcel. Whilst doing his examination he had found a couple of loose apples on the trailer bed. The law states that all loads have to be secure, no matter what their size. These two apples were loose and would have to be removed, an operation he diligently under took. Instead of throwing the fruit to the ground, where in theory he could be accused of dropping litter, he put them in the cab window to be eaten as a snack later on his journey. It was an excuse for the bogies to pounce. To them it was a major crime scene, he'd been caught in the act, and all they wanted me to do was press charges. Bugger off. The apples were technically mine as the load had been signed out of the docks but not signed for at the point of delivery. There is some legal jargon that says they are temporally mine so that I can insure them. It was down to me to press charges but I just laughed. The police could not understand my reasoning or even see the funny side of the occasion.

Over the years I have delivered to most of the London wholesale markets. Due to the nature of their working day this was usually night work or at the very best early morning deliveries. Western International, located just north of Heathrow Airport was a self-help delivery point. The buildings were of simple design being parallel rows of single story lock up units. Each unit was fronted by a roller shutter and occupied by a different wholesaler who would turn up for work at times suited to their individual needs. As a new delivery driver I hoped that they would arrange for a key holder to be present or even to help with the unloading of fruit during the hours of darkness.

My first visit was frustrating. I arrived in the early hours one morning anticipating a greeting by night staff, ready and willing to help off load my trailer. The whole market was dead; a Maris Celeste moment. On finding the industrial unit indicated on my delivery sheet, I parked up and waited. The minutes turned into a couple of hours at which point the adjacent unit sprung into life. I enquired when the tenants of my unit usually arrived. "Not for hours yet drive" was the response to my question. "Tip it yourself." After a polite exchange of words, I discovered many of the units were dummy-locked with the shutters pulled down to give the appearance of security. The visiting driver had to open up and using any available fork truck, make the delivery. I am sure this is a situation that does not often arise today as more goods would leave than would arrive! Opening up the shutter, I was greeted by a well-lit warehouse complete with a tatty electric fork lift. As with many owner drivers of my generation, common sense, self-help and ingenuity saved time and a fortune. I had no bit of paper issued by a training board or college stating that I could operate a fork truck, a certificate organized by some government quirkin having to justify his job. This was to be a self-taught exercise with built in self-assessment. It was not long before the major controls were located and poorly mastered, but the resultant exercise did relieve me of my cargo. Perfection was gained following many visits to the market over the years.

The delivery system in New Covent Garden Market was simple, just book in, drop the trailer with container and pick up empty, exit the market job done.

Spitalfields market near Bank, north of Tower Bridge was probably my favourite market destination. It had a beautiful arena for displaying colourful stalls dripping with fruit and veg. The smell of fresh produce would float on the early morning air. Victorian cast iron columns held up the glass canopy. Traders scurried from stall to stall, porters with hand carts jostled and vied for space in the narrow aisles. The cafés, on the perimeter streets, supplied all the requirements for a working man's stomach. The queues, often spilled out of the doors, like tooth paste. Taxi drivers would join the milling throng of market patrons. On cold mornings the café windows, draped with chequered curtains would steam up, the atmosphere inside would become thick with cigarette smoke and wildly talking men. This situation that could not be repeated today as regulations have decreed we can only smoke outside.

Gone are the days of choice, Big Brother now informs us of our misdoings and punishes any wrong doers. Nice to think there is a faceless person in Whitehall who cares for my well-being. I should be so lucky!

One hot and steamy evening my wife, Chris, accompanied me to the market for the experience. Having explored the local vicinity, White Chapel, the home of Jack the Ripper, we returned to our vehicle to await the arrival of the stall holder. As dusk fell, the street lights flickered into life to cast shadows in doorways. A cat could be heard screeching in an adjacent alley. The sound of a police siren bounced on the evening air reverberating around the market. The sticky evening air bought the ladies of the night out to plunder the pockets of desperate men. I watched with curiosity, as one scantily clad girl approached a car parked in a shadow. She leaned into the driver's window but was obviously rebuked. Chris had dropped off to sleep and was slumped in her seat. Consequently she was unaware of the approaching siren who walked around to my door and looked up. She smiled a sweet innocent smile

"You want business mister?" she asked.

The sound of her voice caused my wife to stir. It was at this point that the girl showed the world just how well blessed she was with womanly attributes! She stood on the step and looked in, about to repeat the question

"Do you want……?" she noticed my wife waking. "Oh! Sorry mate, see you're already fixed." returning to the ground she promptly slipped away into the night like a leaf in a stream.

Borough market lies in the shadow of Southwark Cathedral on the South side of the Thames. Steeped in history, it is possibly the oldest market in London and dates back to the Romans, an edifice to the fruit and veg trade. It only saw my presence once. It is said Shakespeare shopped here and probably visited a localhostelry for a jug of liquid lunch. His Globe Theatre is within easy walking distance.

My mission was to deliver a forty foot trailer to a wholesaler positioned at the rear of the market. Thirty odd years ago, the floor area was cleared every day after trading, thus enabling vehicles to enter and exit the premises. It could take the best part of two days to do one day's work. The trailer had to be delivered during the night before the day of dealing. The stall holders would arrive, set up, and proceed to sell their wares. Subsequently, it became impossible to exit the building until the end of the day's trading.

Today the market is more retail orientated, supplying the local community with fresh produce from the world. The visitor can wallow in the delights of fresh food and tastes. The eye is able to feast on the vivid colours emanating from the stalls, organic food tempting the tree huggers and diet freaks, with cakes or pastries for the rest. Perfume from a million flowers blend with the odour of burgers and tempting smells from Maria's Kitchen. Cheeses from Wales share the same cold cabinet with culinary delights of France and Germany. Exotic fish gawp, mouths wide open, from ice covered counters. The pub, I believe 'The Southwark', on the corner, supplies the natives and tourists alike with a buzzing atmosphere and booze.

Over the road from Borough Market lies Toolley Street and Hays Wharf with their Victorian warehouses backing onto the river. Dark bricks on the waterside were regularly and liberally sprinkled with cross barred windows being reminiscent of a prison. Inside, thick walled halls were encrusted with crates of alcohol from around the planet. These premises have now been rejuvenated into up market 'yuppy' apartments, shops and modern offices. The bonded stores are relegated to wine bars.

My truck and tilt trailer loaded with a thousand cases of French plonk, was destined for one of these warehouses. When the Victorians undertook the construction of the buildings with adjacent quays, the designers were not aware of future juggernauts. Only being used to horse drawn carts and drays, the gates into the yard were narrow. On many occasions, when visiting a new delivery place, I would park up and explore the scene and this time was no exception. The street was heaving with commuters, rushing like ants through a paper straw. Road works meant that the only way in, was to reverse through an awkwardly placed set of cones and road repair plant.

Usually, when you want a copper, there's never one about. When you want a bus you wait and wait, then two come at once. This was a bogey moment a brace of them appeared on cue. These two men were the epitome of what London police men should be, tall, polite and very helpful. Intuitively they read the situation and held back the thronging mass. I had my own police cordon, usually reserved for rioters or football crowds but now earmarked for me. Without hesitation or any word of communication with the two officers, I slowly reversed my vehicle and trailer through the road works and narrow gateway. Inch by inch, without stopping to correct any imperfection, I entered the yard. As the walls of the building closed in, the wing mirrors had to be folded back to prevent damage. Consequently my reversing changed from experience to luck. I missed everything, I did the manoeuvre in one hit, a scenario that usually only occurs when nobody is watching. On this day an impatient baying crowd, eager to continue their journey, was watching. This waiting mob must have been impressed because, on completing the exercise, a round of applause erupted from behind the police line. I felt rather embarrassed but did manage to rise to the occasion and gave a bow from my cab.

Fish gawp from the fish counter and, right, incredible smells from Maria's kitchen.

CHAPTER SEVEN

Police and a wave from the queen

The police have played an important part in my haulage career, some by being considerate and others by being right 'pigs.' Early in the eighties I had the task of delivering steel roofing sheets into Liverpool. The north always seemed wet and cold. Any place above Stratford on Avon is north to me. I thought of this area as the part of England, where the flat cap and pigeons used to be the norm and the place where accents can dictate your status and career. On many occasions I saw wicker baskets full of pigeons, being opened up on the beds of trucks parked in the docks. I would watch, in awe, as the birds rose skywards to circle the area before turning north, no doubt arriving back home to their lofts and food, way before the returning owners.

The last bundle of roofing material had been off loaded at the end of a long day. It was dark-black as an undertaker's hat. I was cold from working on the trailer. If lucky, a quick, hot bite to eat would be followed by a five hour dash home. As the return trip commenced, the rain descended. The wiper blades whacked backwards and forwards comfortingly, a tune that had become familiar. As I entered a roundabout I noticed, in my headlights, a police car parked menacingly, lights out, and on the kerb. On passing I checked my mirrors and the headlights of the police vehicle burst into life. Within a few seconds the car, blue lights flashing, was following me. At a safe place I pulled over and stopped. Nothing happened, they continued to flash. I waited eventually climbing out of my cab to be met by a wall of water from the heavens and spray from passing vehicles. I walked to the rear of my trailer where, soaking wet, I was greeted by a rather burly copper winding his window down.

"You got a bulb gone drive," he shouted. A shower of food sprayed out of his mouth like a Roman candle. I turned and viewed the trailer lights. On each side was a light cluster containing the indicator, side and brake light, one of the bulbs had obviously failed. "Thanks," I replied, "I'll fix it at the services.

"No you won't unless you want a ticket, you'll do it now."

I was getting wetter by the minute. I could see the rain bouncing off the bonnet of their car, like miniature water spouts. The coppers sat back in the dry and watched a very cold and wet driver change the bulb. My vehicle was now, not much safer, having been fitted with one more small bulb, than before. The two police probably felt they were doing their duty. I was very wet, extremely cold and disillusioned. When eventually I sat in my warm cab, vapour could be seen rising from my wet clothes only to condense on the inside of the windscreen to look like fog.

Sometimes an understanding police officer would wander into my working day, one did so during the period after Chris and I had moved to our present house. Our new home was in need of considerable renovation with a new roof, rewiring, and plumbing being urgent jobs to be done. We had to fight rising damp in the walls and rot in the timber floor joists. A few months, if not years of work, lay ahead so consequently, I drove by night and renovated our house by day. Come the middle of the week, tiredness would creep up like a sloth.

One night, when returning from Covent Garden, I fell asleep at the wheel. My slumber was quickly curtailed when the front wheel nuts rattled against the centre barrier, the Armco. The noise sounded like machine gun fire. I awoke with a jerk, and steered back onto the carriage way. Tiredness had caused my brain to condense to mush. It was a point prior to junction 4 of the M3 at Camberley. Without being able to stop I had to continue my journey but soon again found myself in the middle lane. This time travelling at about twenty miles per hour and pondering the reason for white lines. What did they mean? Where should I be? My eye lids were sore with tiredness. If I did not get off the motorway quickly I'd be in the Land of Nod again or worse. Somehow I managed to aim my vehicle off the motorway and stop on the hard shoulder of the slip road. I turned off the engine and on crossing my arms, crashed into deep sleep. My forty winks were, at some point later, interrupted by a flashing blue light shining into my cab. The Old Bill had arrived. There was a knock on the door.

On winding the window down, the police office retorted, "You can't stop here! You'll have to go to the services." These were located about four miles down the road.

"If I go anyplace," I replied, in a slurred voice, "I'll become a death statistic."

There was a quick change of mind from the officer who then replied, "Turn your lights on. Night Night drive, sweet dreams." He returned to his car and departed. Thankfully when daylight burst forth, my vehicle started.

Obviously, driving anything with wheels when wretched with tiredness is never sensible. With a car one can just pull over and kip in a lay by and after a power nap or a longer doze continue the journey. The timing of breaks with heavy vehicles can at times be difficult. In the distant past before tachographs were fitted, dead-lines had to be met, often with the threat of dismissal or loss of contract. Tiredness became the norm. I knew of one large haulage company, now out of business, who would pay cash incentives to drivers to get home every night with no questions asked as to how it was achieved. For my sins I have never knowingly driven over my hours but at times have got very close. If one's week can be planned in advance, breaks can often occur at strange times. Night breaks can fall during daytime or vice versa, a system for maximizing the working week. I recall one such incidence when delivering into London. My working day had finished at about midday; a statuary break was required and taken in Vauxhall.

I love architecture, history and art and often used long break periods to explore, like a tourist, sights and scenes. This particular day the Houses of Parliament seemed fair game. The idea of terrorists or bombs was alien, a reality that had not yet reared its ugly head. The main entrance, opposite Westminster Abbey, was open, a lone policeman stood aimlessly at the door. No concrete crash barriers, no admission fee, no x-ray machines or baggage search, not a whiff of security anywhere. I entered and having passed the time of day with the copper on the gate, I freely wandered through the corridors of power. Time was taken admiring the House of Lords and Commons, I stood in the visitors' gallery which was free of glass screens and gazed at the empty seats of green. The arena for modern democracy, how daunting and exciting. Well known faces passed quickly by me as I repatriated myself to the real world outside.

Once again my stomach requested attention; a course, in the direction of Victoria was taken in the hope of finding a traditional London pub selling pies and a pint. On approaching a set of large open doors set in a high stone wall within a stone's throw of the North entrance of Westminster Abbey I was forced to stop. As I stood on the pavement's edge, a long black limo emerged. To my surprise the occupant's face was familiar, it was her Maj. I waved. She waved back and was driven on. Looking around it became apparent I was her only admirer. She or her clockwork hand had gone out of its way to wave at me. God bless you ma'am.

CHAPTER EIGHT

Fun with a burger van

Night work has always appealed to me as travelling is quicker. The roads are the territory of professionals and I find even radio programs more likable, the hosts, knowing their audience's weird sense of humour. In my early career along with driving I also found time to work as a bus fitter, with the nights being most leisurely. If you understood the system it was always possible to find time to work on our own jobs or jobs for friends. Tea breaks seemed to be more frequent. Meals were often of the 'take away' nature. I remember one particular night, when it was my turn to get the burgers. As part of a bus service plan, having done all the checks, the repairs plus adjustments, all buses had to be road tested. "Nicholls!" the night charge hand erupted, "When you have finished that bus, see what everyone wants and get the grub in." A quick scout around the depot furnished me with a catalogue of burger requirements, ketchup with this, onions with that, some with cheese, others with pineapple plus endless cans of drinks. My list looked like a school register of foreign kids.

The number of mobile eateries at two in the morning was somewhat limited. I chose one, a little off the beaten track, or should I say a bus route. With the list safely stowed in my pocket I ventured into the dark of the night for a test drive and the food mercy dash. About two miles from the depot and a mile from my rendezvous with the burger van, a blue light appeared in my mirror. I slowed to let him past. He promptly did and pulled up sharply in front of me. At least the bus brakes worked well. Out slithered a copper. He put his cap on and approached my bus.

"What you doing with this bus?" he enquired.

This to me was a daft question, a test drive and a meal deal. I quickly assumed in my infinite wisdom that he thought I had nicked the vehicle. This could be fun.

"Getting burgers," I replied.

"You being funny son?" replied the man in blue.

"No, it's my turn."

"What you mean?" replied the copper. I got the impression he was getting a little annoyed.

"I've just serviced this vehicle and am taking it for a test drive. I've been elected to buy the burgers."

"If you don't mind son, we will escort you."

True to his word he followed me. I led him the long, pretty route around the town. To be honest my instructions were to do a test drive which I conscientiously did and eventually arrived at the burger van, only to wait in a queue before purchasing the food. The copper maintained his watch on me from the comfort of his motor. I gave a courteous wave and lingering grin before setting off for the trip back to the depot. The route back was short as the priority was not to let the burgers get cold! The police car followed, like a limpet, into the workshop to block off my exit. The foreman approached with the cry.

"Where you been Nicholls?"

The policeman clambered from his car and sauntered over to the foreman.

"You know this lad?"

"Yes, why, what's he done?"

51

"He said he was getting in the burgers."

"That's right and he took his bloody time."

I've never seen a police car turn round and leave so quickly.

CHAPTER NINE

Red Ted and his bath

I think Red Ted was the third driver to join the cause. He was a short, dumpy man with a thick neck and a brilliant red face, his nick name, was derived from his politics rather than the broken blood vessels in his cheeks. A staunch Labour follower, capable of instructing anybody on how to run their business, so long as he didn't have to take any responsibility for his actions. A house owner and member of the local golf club in which, upon his retirement, he bought shares and played out the remaining years of his life. Ted was a familiar face around the docks, well, often wearing his trilby, slightly cocked to the right. To a stranger he had the demeanour of Arthur Daily, car dealer and general wide boy. His extremely militant ways made it difficult for him to find employment, but when working for me, his manner was that of a true gentleman.

It was at this point I invested, or to be honest the bank did on my behalf, in my first second hand Volvo F88, with a 290 lump and a sixteen speed gear box. For the first time, the driver's comfort took priority over the boss's need for economy. She was fast, grabbing the road like shit to a blanket. This princess among trucks could cruise at seventy, fully laden and still return eight to the gallon, I could load twenty ton of concrete kerb stones out of Halifax and be tipping in Southampton, four hours later. It is difficult do the same journey time today in a car. This beautiful truck, only three years old, with half a million miles on the clock became my Swedish girl-friend. We were inseparable for the best part of fourteen years as I watched her age graciously and saw her mileage creep to over two and a half million. She was never an old dog, only a lady. To this day she often appears in my dreams I have either lost her or am standing on the brakes hoping she will stop. This is the point I always wake up with a cold sweat.

Red Ted thus inherited my old AEC. He never complained. I did not like to miss out on technological progress and I proceeded to convert, one week end, the cab into a sleeper. Although functional, it would not have achieved public adoration at a truck show. It would have been more acceptable at the Bath and West Agricultural Show. The well-proportioned lines of the cab extension, gave the appearance of a chicken house. I understand Ted never used the facilities offered by this cab.

It is a well-known tradition, almost a rite of passage, that many drivers feel it is their contractual duty to fiddle their employer. It could be a diesel swindle when some of the fuel being syphoned off with a few drops for sale or for the running of the driver's own car. The selling of extra pallets was another way of making extra cash. Some drivers just stole some of the load. Ted's escapade was doing 'dodgies'. He would spread out the time he spent at a delivery point in order to gain a night out. Friday would be a prime target with an extra bonus of five hours wages for a 'run in' on a Saturday, usually having done only two hours' work. His misdemeanour was brought to light very early on in his career, when he was accidentally bubbled by another driver. I did not have the heart to confront him, but kept an eye on his activities. I know of one driver who managed so many dodgy nights out in one particular car-park in Bristol, so that he could meet up with a lady friend, that his fellow drivers' successfully sent him a birthday card addressed to his truck.

Ted was employed on container work which involved collection, delivering and then returning the box to the docks. He was paid by the mile plus delays and nights out. This system favoured the haulier and driver but cost the shipping company a small fortune. It was a short lived practise to be replaced by a job rate, but while it lasted the hauliers maximized their returns. As far as I was concerned, I was happy so long as the vehicle made money, Ted could play his little games. He would regularly run out of time, usually at a service station about fifty or sixty miles from base. A cadged lift from another driver would return Ted to the comfort of his own bed. Early the following morning, he would hitch back to his motor, hoping that, on his return, the batteries or wheels had not been stolen. At the end of the week, a claim for a night out would be filed. It was only fair. He had gone to all that trouble and wasted his own time, he deserved rewarding! What he failed to realize was that I was also being paid.

Friday was pay day. I knew where he would be, at home in the bath. I must be the only boss in the world who has hand delivered a pay packet to a driver in his wash tub. I would be welcomed by his wife and shown upstairs. Without fail, the bathroom door would be ajar with steam spewing through the crack like dragon's breath. The heat was stifling, immediately I would start sweating and my shirt would cling to my back as if I'd been frog marched through the Brazilian jungle.

Ted was predictable- "Come in Chris, have a drink."

Every week a new bottle of Scottish Whisky would be perched precariously at the end of the boiling bath, along with a spare tumbler. No doubt the latter housed his teeth at night, but now it would accommodate a tipple. He would sit up and commence to pour my drink before settling back into the deep waters, to glow like a sunburnt walrus. The intense heat and bath salts from Ted's cauldron would bite at the rear of my mouth, a sip of the malt doing little to soothe the pain. I believe my love of the Scottish brew started in Ted's bathroom. For about an hour he would give me a breakdown of his weekly woes and how he would change the country if he had Maggie's (Thatcher) job. As a strong supporter of the other side, he would have been a Man. United fan rather than Man. C. out of principle and loyalty to colour of the shirt.

One foggy morning, before I began my day's driving, I received the dreaded phone call. It was Ted, "I've broken down" he said.

"Where?" was my instant response.

"Just after Fleet Services."

For the uninitiated, this is the motorway services between Winchester and London.

"The engine started to make a knocking noise, so I stopped," he continued.

"You didn't drive far did you? I asked anxiously.

"No!"

"Good, go back and wait, I'll come up."

If I was lucky I might be able to save the engine but, as it turned out, once again luck had deserted me. I believe that everybody has a guardian angel; some people are blessed with a 'lucky mate'. If I have one, he or she often goes AWOL, usually at a critical time.

I changed my plans for the day, made a hasty journey to my workshop where I collected every tool I had ever owned. Before I made the drive to Fleet, I made a detour to the local AEC agent and purchased a set of 'big end shells'. The morning sun failed to completely lift the fog, it was destined to be a nice day however at this point the hard shoulder looked wet, cold and forbidding. On arrival at Fleet I gave my car keys to Ted and bade him farewell as he headed for home.

The morning was spent stripping down the engine replacing end shells and doing a major re-build on the hard shoulder of the M3. Not once did the Old Bill stop to question my activities. Today if you stop, the plastic police, sorry, motorway officers in their Chelsea tractors, will descend like vultures to investigate your problem then retire to a safe position to sit and watch. The only occasion when I have found them useful was one warm summer's day when a gorgeous, well-proportioned, young lady, had a flat front tyre. Two officers had stripped to their waists, and with yellow jackets thrown to one side were replacing the wheel! I'm sure unless I had had

56

implants and re-structuring, I would have waited until the end of time for the same care. It would be impossible to do an engine re-build in the same place today. Nowadays, the owner would receive a very large invoice for having a wrecker drag the offending vehicle to a garage.

With the job completed, old oil returned to the engine, I fired up the beast. Perfect! It ticked over and ran as sweet as a nut. I was covered in oil but that didn't matter as the engine sounded fine, I felt great. This feeling of contentment lasted for about thirty miles before the knocking noise returned, and by the time I reached Southampton its tune had changed to a banging sound with pedestrians turning in wonderment!

Ted was informed of the untimely death of his truck on my return. I explained that a new truck would be coming his way. His little, round, red face gleamed with excitement at the prospect and Ted spent days boasting to his mates in the docks, that Nicholls was going to get him a new truck. Imagine his disappointment when an old A series ERF turned up. It was a simple misunderstanding, a play on words. I failed to mention that it would be a new truck to me, but at the same time, a well-worn one! Ted, for reasons known only to him, quit shortly after being introduced to his new vehicle!

CHAPTER TEN

Irish John

Irish John was a delightful man who managed to charm our daughter into playing her recorder at his wedding. Personally at the time, although conscientious and loyal, I considered him as sharp as a brick and as bright as a wickless candle. If I have misjudged him due to the lack of deep conversations, I do apologize. He was taken on as part of yet another expansion experiment which unfortunately ended in disaster! The shipping company, United States Line had decided to use the port of Southampton as their UK base. I believe most of their work, if not all, was supplying American bases with American goods the products coming in all forms from food to aircraft hardware. These out posts, embedded in the English countryside from Berkshire to Lincolnshire, were serviced daily by container. Irish John was my contribution to world peace and the Cold War.

For over a year his F88 became a regular feature of the docking bays of Mildenhall and Greenham Common. However, over time, as the American Forces slowly relinquished their hold on our countryside, his services were required less and less and eventually the job ceased. Other forms of work were undertaken by John whilst I looked for alternative haulage work. During one quiet week he dug a soak away for one of our properties, following instructions he produced a hole about eight feet square by eight feet deep. I don't know whether the handling of a spade was an inborn gene inherited from his Irish roots, but the perfect result seemed unnatural. I think, with our John, the holding of a shovel gave him the same pleasure as a child holding a stick of Blackpool Rock. At the end of the day a cuboid, honed to perfection, greeted me. All I had wanted was a rough hollow but if I'd had an eight foot Rubic Cube it would have dropped into the hole and fitted like a glove.

Other transport opportunities were sought. A newly formed roofing material distributor, with whom I had a nodding acquaintance, was looking for a small haulier to distribute its products. I was their man and Irish John was mine. I hired a brick crane trailer and duly trained Jon in safety procedures. Professional courses in the handling of Hiabs weren't available at that time so, as I'd had a certain amount of skill gained from experience with my own vehicle I did my best to share my knowledge. His first job proved disastrous, resulting in a very large invoice from the hire company. John had managed to smash the mast and loading arm into a railway bridge in Aylesbury thus ending his dabble into crane work! Also, within the following six months, he had turned an oblong container into a diagonally shaped box after hitting a bridge! My accumulated brownie points with one of the world's largest shipping companies were lost due to the resulting damage even though I'd worked tirelessly for them for many years without any problems! This latest misadventure was quickly followed by my gift to John of his P45 after which he repatriated himself back to Ireland.

The quest for profit or a good living resulted in working though most bank holidays. The Boxing Day following Irish John's misdemeanour was no exception, a brownie point collection exercise in an effort to regain my lost credit with the shipping company. An over height, twenty foot container was required in Grangemouth for customer delivery in the few days between Christmas and New Year. I had the job of trunking north from Southampton which was an uneventful journey on near empty roads. On reaching my destination, I dropped the loaded trailer and picked up an empty forty foot skelly for the return. All progressed well for a few miles until I reached the fire station when my cab filled with thick black, odorous smoke! Five hundred miles from home, a bank holiday and fire trouble had followed me over the border. At a guess my problems were electrical, caused by the recently picked-up trailer. If I was correct, the shipping company could pick up the tab. A quick disconnection of the batteries saw an instant decline in the volume of smoke. The tell-tale signs of melted cables confirmed the source of the problem. After waiting an hour, the cab was cleared of fumes and I continued my journey home. The great thing about old diesel engines is that once started, an electrical supply is not required. A few seconds of power from the battery, before disconnection, produced a living engine. I travelled only during daylight hours, cautiously braking when a vehicle was behind me in order to prevent a rear end shunt. Without any electrics I had no indicators or lights, a reversion to hand signals was the only form of communication I had. It was a blessing the Christmas break had seen a dramatic drop in road vehicles. Once safely back in Southampton, my theory of the cause of the problem was confirmed by the contractors used to service Southampton based trailers.

"You were lucky your cab didn't catch fire, that trailer's fucked," was the statement I was hoping to hear.

The depot manager disagreed, but when informed that the trailer was from Scotland, he smiled and said, "That's OK then. Get a quote for a new loom from Volvo and Scotland can pay the bill!"

A couple of hours of work, splicing in new cables and connectors to by-pass the damaged loom, put my vehicle back on the road. It was a patchwork of wires, hopefully to be professionally replaced in the near future with a new loom. The quote was subsequently presented and it was a three day wait before my wife received a call from the shipping companies head office in London. A foul mouthed gentleman, swearing and cursing, informed her that the invoice for the damage done to our truck would not be paid! It was a conversation that left her crying and shaking. I thought of legal action, but without financial backing this option was short lived. We were never again offered any work from this shipping company, no doubt a case of two strikes and you were out, stuff your years of loyal help. If I was paying back handers or doing favours for traffic handlers, like many hauliers were, the outcome might have been different.

Princess with brick crane trailer and Irish John's unit.

CHAPTER ELEVEN

The yard and giving the copper a good hiding

The yard, as we call it, was a gift from heaven. It replaced the field I was using as a workshop. At times it became the hub of my social scene, an oasis in Southampton from where I hoped to expand and put my haulage business on a more professional footing. When I was first shown the estate by Snoop Dog the owner, I was relieved to find somewhere close to home with a reasonable rent and from where I could pursue my dreams. The entrance was via a pair of high, blue painted gates, located between two houses which were just wide enough to take a commercial vehicle. Having passed through this access, the yard opened up to form a large, L shaped expanse. It had been a derelict coal yard, scattered with an assortment of old rusting corrugated iron lock-up garages, the odd shed, a port-a-cabin plus barn and a few disused pig sties. It was a wild ram shackled paradise for kids and a place where my enthusiasm for life and business could expand.

Before long I became acquainted with the tenants, a cross section of 'would be' entrepreneurs. Snoop Dog, with his side kick, young Doris, real name Dennis, ran a garage from a group of three lock-ups. 'There and Back' taxis holed up in a shed, close to the gates. Kevin the fish man conducted his Saturday night pub delivery enterprise from the rear of refrigerated van. The vehicle was a wreck but the body still worked as a freezer! Ginger, the Corona agent used one of the lock-ups for the storage of aerated pop. The boys James and John Taylor ran their scrap, now known as a recycling business, from another. At the top of the yard stood the barn complete with straw and an abandoned Thames Trader, if my memory serves me correctly. This flat-bed vehicle was bestrewn with cobwebs and was a rotting hulk, the galloping rust bug having taken revenge. To the left of the barn were the pig sties, a small group of concrete pens that screamed with potential. The latter were to be my base, my operating centre and H.Q.

Over the years the yard expanded and moved on to become a small industrial estate. Snoop Dog's garage moved to the barn to become an M.O.T. test station. The lock-up garages were demolished, replaced by small industrial units, but its character has never changed. My efforts to turn the piggeries into a work shop marked the start of changes to the yard. Weekends and days off from driving were spent knocking down walls and heightening others to produce a workshop capable of housing one truck. An office, complete with the ever boiling kettle, took pride of place at the rear. The thin, dirt floor was replaced by a foot thick pad of concrete. A friend, who was an owner driver, had changed from general hire and reward with his flatbed to a contract hauling with a truck mixer and became an ideal supplier of concrete. This was an instance where the initiative of a driver could be rewarding, excess concrete being sold on as a driver perk. Failure to empty and clean the vehicle at the end of the day would produce solid sediment within a few hours. A cost conscious driver had a list of potential customers willing to accept a yard or so.

A new floor for the workshop was required so three yards was ordered with six yards of rapidly drying product arriving! A quick round up of potential helpers produced three. As the drum turned, concrete disgorged from its gaping mouth to gather in an ever growing pyramid. As we shovelled, pushed and pulled the mound around the floor, we could feel the rapidly drying chemical contained within the mix, kick in. The heat rose, the concrete began to set, sweat from my brow dripped incessantly to the wet floor as the pace quickened in an effort to get it laid before going completely off. The temperature grew inside my boots leaving me with second degree burns on my ankles and billowing, yellow blisters on my feet, not a lot of fun, especially when they finally burst!

Unexpectedly, and possibly an unwelcome surprise to Jim, was the copper who took up residence in the port-a-cabin. Jim considered the Police to be one of life's challenges, an inconvenience to be tolerated but not befriended. The Bogie, as he was called, although not affectionately was treated with suspicion by most at the yard. Jim would often refer to him by his collective noun for police as a 'snot '. This yard bogie had been demoted, why I do not know, but he did boast of planting evidence if he considered a suspected criminal guilty. The day he retired he was beaten up and given a good kicking. His face took on the appearance of a Domino's pizza. I understand he never reported the perpetrator or perpetrators. It was generally considered his list of friends could only be counted when he looked in a mirror.

One particular, memorable day I was undertaking repairs to one of my vehicles but nothing was going right. I was hungry, cursing and had a fraying temper. I remembered the cab was tilted to expose the engine and chassis. Whilst bending over the front wheel, trying to replace a worn airline, the Bogie thought it amusing to creep up behind me and grab my genitalia. I would have no problems with females doing the latter, but a male, no way! His grin changed instantly to a wince and a cry as I spun around and lunged at him. I was holding a twelve inch adjustable spanner at the time and this lump of steel was launched with full ferocity at the nearest part of his body. I split the back of his hand open from his wrist to knuckle. No doubt it was common assault, but I considered it was self-defence. Blood squirted from the wound to come to rest on his suit. His high-pitched scream produced a small number of spectators. Upon knowing the facts, they smiled, congratulated me before returning to their relevant jobs. The Bogie slunk away never to converse with me again. I could not have hoped for a better out-come.

During the period I was at the yard my engineering skills were pushed to the limit. Remember, I was not time served or qualified in anyway. My abilities grew through experience and learning by my mistakes. I must have become competent because the local Volvo truck dealership often picked my brains when trouble shooting F88 problems. On a number of occasions I was offered a full time job in their workshop. Apart from the servicing and repairing of other companies' vehicles I undertook a number of my own projects. My first and favourite F88 had only two axles. The government at the time, in order to come into line with European requirements, increased the carrying capacity of artic HGV vehicles from 32ton to 38ton. The proviso being the extra weight had to be carried on an extra axle. In order to keep my Volvo and take advantage of the new regulations a third axle would have to be fitted. The prices charged by the specialist companies undertaking such modifications were prohibitive. Self-help, as usual, was the order of the day, a task I relished at the time but would not consider today. The fifth wheel had to be removed, the chassis cut and a double-axle from a second hand Scania tipper, spliced in. A new sliding fifth wheel was consequently fitted.

Jim supplied a set of stainless steel lift doors redundant from a local hospital refurbishment. These became a very presentable set of rear mudguards. An integral part of a Vulcan Bomber that Taylor boys were scrapping at the time was incorporated into the vertical exhaust stack behind the cab. This stack could produce perfect smoke rings when started on a cold morning. Later, as the vehicle got older, the exhaust smoke became denser until the engine warmed up. On at least two occasions the copious amount of smoke, caused members of the public to phone the fire brigade! Finally a new vehicle MOT made the rig road legal. The bonus of the Scania axle was the inclusion of lifting facilities. The ability of the driver to lift the trailing axle from inside his cab could be advantageous in icy conditions, the procedure produced more traction. A perfect solution when distributing propane gas bottles to customers whose premises were often off the beaten track. The latter was a job I undertook for many years until global warming greatly reduced the winter demand for bottled gas.

When fitting the lifting axle a smidgen of creative engineering was demanded. An understanding of basic hydraulics could allow phenomenal lifting capabilities to be achieved. A twenty four volt pump put oil into two ex-fork truck rams. I could lift fifteen tons of trailer one foot into the air at a flick of a switch. I was so impressed by my own skills that if an occasion arose to show off the trucks capabilities, I would take full advantage of the moment. One such excuse presented itself in Norman Offer's yard, just outside Southampton dock gates. Norman, possibly the most likeable, well dressed haulage contractor in the area, hailed me as I entered his yard. He had obviously heard from one of his drivers Nicholls had stretched his Volvo. He looked impressed and bent down to take a closer look at the operating system just at the second I commenced to engage lift mode. Such was the high working pressure of the equipment that a hose fractured sending a fountain of pink oil cascading over Norman, covering his face, his neck and what looked like a brand new suit! Being the gentleman he was, he failed to explode and took the accident in good spirits. Twenty plus years later, his son remembers the day with affection.

The other major projects involved the modifications of two trailers. One was to reduce, a bog standard thirty five foot tri-axle trailer to a thirty foot tank container trailer complete with product pump and container front end lifting gear. The other started life as twin axle, thirty foot, general purpose, flat-bed trailer. On completing the modifications it became a centre mounted brick crane trailer complete with drop down sides. The main reason for this endeavour was for the distribution of Spanish slates. The final job, before putting this project back on the road, was to apply a coat or two of paint. A suitable warm day was chosen. The trailer was centrally placed in the yard so access to all parts of the chassis could easily be gained. I used the truck's own compressor to supply high pressure air to the spray gun. With the reservoir suitably filled with black paint, I commenced and finished painting the chassis. I thought I had done a fantastic job and it looked 'the doggies'. On extracting myself from under the trailer I was met by Doris, absolutely wetting him-self with laughter.

"You twat, Nicholls!" he exclaimed, "Have you seen Ginger's car?"

"No," I replied. I looked in disbelief. Ginger, our Corona agent, had just taken delivery of a brand new cherry red vehicle. When I say new, I mean he had collected it two days earlier. This gleaming example of Japanese motor technology now looked like a carnival float, a giant red and black ladybird. The spray-off had been taken by the wind to settle on the motor. Ginger was not available for comment at the time and I have waited to this day for him to complain. Doris has recently informed me that he charged Ginger, £30 for 'mopping' the auto!

CHAPTER TWELVE

Yard outings

The yard social scene was the brain child of Doris. This young man, pumped high with testosterone, took it upon himself to organize 'gentleman's evenings'. It was difficult to work out which was bigger, his ego or libido. He has always been quick witted with a healthy amount of cynicism. He and Jim, our yard scrap merchant, had one thing in common they were both as honest as they could afford to be. Years of experience as a car salesman afforded Doris the ability to convince any unsuspecting member of the public, that the bit of junk, sorry, the dream making machine he was trying sell at the time, was the best buy in town. Bullshit always baffles the best of brains.

Gentlemen's evenings, occurred a couple of times a year, either in the local rugby club or a back room of a pub. Apart from the décor and location, all the evenings were organised on similar lines with booze, food, a blue comic and a stripper or two. These provided the perfect ingredients for a yard full of studs, even if only in their dreams! In order to maximize profits or just to break even, friends, customers and acquaintances were welcome so long as the appropriate entrance fee was forthcoming. All occasions were well attended and very boisterous. The blue comics often met their match from members of a quick witted audience who would heckle or yell remarks back with annoying frequency. This back lash added to the amusement of the goading spectators. The blue comic's stage time was considerably increased by the repeated use of the 'f' word. This is one of the few words in the English language that functions as noun, adjective and verb. All forms of the 'f' word were included in every sentence. The 'f' word has, over years, slotted into every day speech without causing disturbance but when uttered from a stage it generates hoots of laughter. This resembles the 'naughty boy syndrome' of school bus humour when the Oxford Dictionary was explored, grubby pages being turned to find wicked words like 'nude' or 'virgin'. Who would have guessed that Richard Branson would turn one into an internationally respected brand?

The occasion that has stayed deep in my memory, was the evening I was picked on. Pete, the friend who had accompanied me to Switzerland, Mike my faithful driver and I had been persuaded to attend an evening of live entertainment. The Antony Arms, a seedy establishment, on its 'last legs' was the chosen watering hole. The venue was to be the committee room on the first floor. On ascending the scrubbed wooden stairs at the end of a dingy hall, we were confronted by a pair of shabby swinging doors. As every patron entered, the hinges cried out for oil. Once inside, the gloom of the poorly painted, intimate room made its presence known. Damaged curtains hung from the sullied windows at one end. Below the window, half a dozen or so rows of grey plastic chairs provided the seating. At the opposite end of the room, a low, make shift stage was obviously to be the centre of entertainment. Against the wall, facing the door was the bar and food stall. The bar contained two barrels, one of lager, one of beer. No doubt the casks were close to, or past their sell by date, and operated by the young Doris. He dispatched alcohol in plastic glasses until both butts were dry. Snacks the usual pub fare adorned a wall paper paste table. Armed with a disposable plateful and a pint each, Pete, Mike and I took refuge in the middle of the back row. Hopefully this move would put us out of reach of the girls, who would often make there naked bodies at home amongst the audience.

Doris, now forsaking his duties as publican, became the master of ceremonies. As the stage lights, a couple of light bulbs screwed to a plank, burst into life, he cordially thanked all for attending the' happening' and invited us to listen to the comic. He was a Londoner, keen to take the piss out of us lads. His script, intertwined with smut and the all too present 'f' word, was not well received. His career in Southampton was short lived and he was booed and jeered off the stage. The main act, the reason why we lads had parted with the queen's silver, appeared. Three, twenty something girls dressed in very little, performed their gyrating dance routine on a small grubby rug to the sound of the usual tune, 'The Stripper'. Slowly, as each article of dress was slowly removed, these ladies became acquainted with the cold air of the room. Goose pimples could readily be seen rising on their young flesh. With the discarding of every piece of clothing the blood temperature of the all-male onlookers increased. Cheers of delight and wolf whistles echoed around the room. These girls were a considerable success unlike the comic.

One of the girls, now only wearing make-up, jumped from the low stage. She made her way into the crowd carrying a beer mug into which was heaped coins from satisfied punters. Doris followed close behind, almost as if glued to her. He always wanted to be near the action and closely following the girl suited him well. As she approached our seating area, Doris pointed to me and cried in a voice for all to hear,

"Nicholls will do, he's the one who wants to join the army when he grows up."

In my mid–thirty's, I often wore government surplus clothes, either dark blue or khaki. On this occasion my dress code was indeed, khaki. She approached me, grabbed my collar with her free hand and proceeded to drag me from my seat. Pete and Mike were possibly relieved they were to be spared the humiliation. Making a fuss or refusing would have been more embarrassing! The crowd of lads did their best to cheer and push me toward the stage. As I approached the podium we were joined by the two other girls. Between them they hauled me to centre stage. Cheers from the now wailing crowd over powered the music. Men left their seats to place themselves closer to the stage and gain a better view of the entertainment. Slowly those three girls stripped me of every item of attire! My clothes, piece by piece were held aloft and swung around their heads then released to fly serenely to all parts of the stage. The roars of laughter from an excited audience must have been heard in the street below. This mortifying experience lasted a few minutes after which the girls picked up a beer mug each and commenced to circulate among the lads in an endeavour to fill their glasses with more cash. The subject of their entertainment, namely yours truly, was left to find his clothes. I assume, it has never been confirmed, Doris with his wicked sense of humour, had picked up my entire outfit and hidden it. I spent the best part of five minutes parading around the stage bollock naked searching cupboards and behind curtains in an effort to be reunited with them. Eventually holding my garments in front of me as if to protect my balls I was hauled to front of stage by Doris. With a few choice words and a round of applause from the audience he thanked me for my pathetic performance. I suppose I was expected to rise to the occasion.

"Well done Nicholls," whispered Doris. "I didn't think you would survive."

Over the years, ventures into Europe also became regular interludes to the everyday tedium of the yard. Booze cruises near Christmas and summer, excursions to stock our cupboards with tobacco and alcohol. On one occasion, in November 1986, we took part in the Beaujolais run to raise funds for a local special school in need of a new swimming pool. Our efforts involved cycling in relay, day and night, as slowly as possible from Macon in France back to England. This jaunt into foreign lands was followed the next year with the hiring of a motor cruiser on a French canal in Brittany. These excursions were a cross between 'Three men in a Boat' and 'The Canterbury Tales' a boat load of incidences and adventures that could warrant a book of their own.

Participant sports have never been on my list of hobbies, even fishing, possibly the least demanding of physical activities has never appealed. At school, footer was the main recreation for the boys. My lack of enthusiasm must have been apparent as I was always designated the position of goalie, probably because I was useless as a striker or defender or in hindsight maybe it was because I was always getting in the way! I tried cricket once, but there again luck more than skill was my friend. I was pulled in as a reserve to play against another school. When fielding I found myself looking into the sun and had little view of the ball. When the shout of "Look out," erupted from the coach, I looked up to see a black round shape rapidly approaching. I cupped my hands in defence of my face and the ball crashed into my awaiting palms, my fingers clenched in an involuntary action-behold, I had the only catch of the day!

As Snoop Dog the yard owner grew older, he became a health freak. Rolling his own fags, one of the reasons for our visits to France was given up and a healthy diet pursued. Exercise, in the way of golf, seemed to fit well into his new world. The yard golf team was fleetingly formed. A few rounds at the local municipal course were subsequently organized until it was recognized that I was the handicap.

CHAPTER THIRTEEN

The wheels fall off

Heavy vehicle design and technology has progressed out of all recognition during my driving career with the exception of the problem of wheel security unless you call fitting bright yellow marker arrows progress.

When I started driving heavy trucks, women HGV drivers were as rare as hens-teeth. In order to pull the non-power assisted steering wheel or operate a clutch devoid of air assistance, they would have had to be built like a butcher's dog or a Russian weight lifter. Today, any girl, however petite and who can scale the steps to the cab is able to handle the largest of monster trucks with ease. The hardest part of driving a modern truck is setting the heater temperature and adjusting the arm rests.

Wheel safety has changed little with the passing of time for units and trailers or rigids. My first encounter with a wheel problem was with an ERF. Mike Irons had the job of delivering a forty foot container, loaded with iceberg lettuces to Swanley in Kent. On the previous day, I had a set of four new tyres fitted by a national tyre company to the rear axle of the vehicle. Having loaded the box, complete with a heavy, built-in refrigeration plant at the front end, Mike proceeded to make his way to the delivery point. The M25 had not been built if my memory serves me correctly so old A roads were the order of the day. Just prior to Swanley was a dog legged railway bridge. Entering the bridge with the load proved easy but on exiting through the arch, the dynamics of the load put extra pressure on the offside rear wheels and axle. The resultant transfer of weight sheered all ten wheel studs from the wheel drum. Nuts and studs became air born and the two wheels parted company with the axle. Now liberated, the pair headed for freedom. One careered straight ahead to be recaptured when it came to rest at the kerb side while the other was last seen entering a corn field at high speed never to be seen by us again. I can only assume the farmer on harvesting the crop would have possibly found it when it probably wrecked the cutting table of his combine! As a result of this incident, the tyre company, which had fitted the new tyres the previous day, changed their fitting procedures to include torqueing the nuts to a specific tension. This was supposed to alleviate all future problems of over tightening with the windy gun.

Time is money in transport. 'Bread' can only be made when the wheels are turning. There is a delicate balance between wearing the vehicle out with the consequential costs and driving it to oblivion for maximum return. The returning of the above damaged vehicle to a productive state was surprisingly quick. On discussing the breakdown with Mike over the phone, I dispensed with the usual technique of organizing a wrecker to tow the offending vehicle to local garage and decided on a road side repair. A couple of phone calls found the location of a scrapyard breaking a similar vehicle to mine and could supply a spare brake drum and a set of nuts. The family estate car, still laden with the weekly shopping and child seats was commandeered. Loaded with tools and a spare tyre I set off, via thescrap yard for Swanley. The cold store had dispatched its own tug to retrieve the trailer and unload the lettuce. On arriving at my listing truck, Mike and I made short work of replacing the offending brake drum. In under an hour the ERF was again road worthy and in earning mode.

The other major episode involving the loss of tyres was a number of years later when I owned my beloved F88. Again a new set of tyres had recently been fitted to the drive axle. My contract was to deliver three loads of cheese to a cold store in Somerset, in all, a two day job. The night out was taken just outside Wincanton in the truck park of the old Frying Pan. The evening was hot and sticky, my shirt stuck to my back like my wife's cakes to a baking tin. The thought of greasy food and the boredom of my own company seemed an unbearable prospect. A managerial decision was made and I decided on a cold evening meal and a long cool pint in a country pub. A possible natter to a local would be fitting reward for a good day's graft. The hostelry was located about a mile from my chosen resting place. A brisk walk brought me to the comfort of this village tavern. Beams, low ceilings bejewelled with copper artefacts met the visiting traveller.

It was some hours later and after a very pleasant meal, I returned through the chilly night air to my cab for a well-earned sleep. As dawn broke the early morning sun greeted me by piercing through the curtains to shine fiercely into my eye. God's own wake-up call that beats any alarm clock. Having washed and consumed a hearty, if not unhealthy, breakfast in the' Frying Pan', I continued my return trip back to the docks to pick up the third load of cheese. Just shy of Mere, two young females stood at the road side trying to hitch a lift. My fatherly instinct kicked in, I felt girls alone on a major road could in danger. In the seventies and eighties truck drivers were considered 'Knights' of the road and thus a certain amount of responsibility was thrust upon us to do the right thing. Today I would hesitate to give a lift to anybody except a Trade Plater. The repercussions from a disingenuous, non-paying passenger could lead to a potential nightmare. Nowadays possible negative accusations or even the chance of being robbed, blight the good nature of the average driver. Unfortunately the ever present threat of dismissal often leads distressed damsels being left at the kerb side.

The two girls looked delighted that I had pulled up. A lift in a lorry would have seemed a bit of a novelty and conversation piece on returning home. I leaned over to the passenger door, and upon opening it, one looked up and said, "Salisbury?""Yes," I replied and grabbed the back pack which was being pushed into my face. With a twist of the wrist it came to rest on my bunk. The girls, now impatient, commenced to climb the steps and tumble like falling logs onto the passenger seat. Within a few moments we were on our way but I soon became aware these girls were French. As my knowledge of their language can be written on the back of a postage stamp, our conversation was limited. They took out their map and jabbering together, proceeded to study it intently.

For a while the journey was uneventful, a joyous jaunt through the Wiltshire countryside. The early morning sun and the music from my radio made for a wondrous beginning to the day. All seemed well until I was passed by two truck wheels, black wheels, my back wheels and they were heading into the distance. These large spinning discs had developed lives of their own. They were like a couple of ballroom dancers, doing the same moves but equal and opposite, a male and female with their own agenda. They weaved in unison, parted company and returned together. To my horror a green Mini-Clubman came into view. I watched helplessly as these two wheels crossed the white line. Like an Exocet missile they seemed targeted on the mini. Time seemed to sink into slow motion. A million thoughts rushed through my head, not one of them reassuring. As I slowed to a halt, my eyes stayed transfixed on the wheels. All I can say is my guardian angel must have had one hell of a wake-up call. The two wheels separated to pass on each side of the mini. I do not believe the two old ladies inside, complete with hats akimbo saw the wheels from beginning to end. There again they could have been struck ridged with fear! What-ever the reason they did not veer from a straight course. As I stopped, the two French girls, who must have been watching the incident unfold, did a runner. Not even a 'Merci' or an 'Au revoir' was heard. How ungrateful - I blame their parents or was it just a Frog thing? All evidence of them travelling with me vanished bar a French map of England. This sheet of paper still has a place on my book shelf.

Dripping with sweat and with relief I ran the course of the two escapee tyres. Their dance routine must have continued to the very end as they had both lovingly come to rest together. On inspection, nine wheel nuts were still in the rim. Bugger, I had lost one. At the junction of the A303 and the A36 stood a garage, this was my next destination on foot as I had failed to carry a jack strong enough to lift the axle and trailer. On enquiring as to the possibility of borrowing one, the garage owner insisted I should leave a deposit. I returned to my vehicle, replaced the wheels with all nuts minus the one I couldn't find. Less than a couple of hours after picking up the two French girls I was on my way again and possibly a stone lighter. A conversation with the tyre company led to consensus of opinion that robbery was the motive. On returning from my evening meal in the country pub I had disturbed thieves trying to steal my tyres! Well that was their story.

CHAPTER FOURTEEN

Regulations and saving a life.

Big brother in Europe has, over the years, produced some regulations for English drivers to follow to the letter and for the French to be used as guide lines. One particular set, pertaining to the carriage of hazardous substances, included information on first aid procedures. For years whether driving my F88 or later the Mercedes, I have regularly collected or delivered liquid products in and out of Fawley Refinery. For years I have handled tons of bottled propane gas during winter months. Potentially, both situations could be considered problematic. For the owner driver or small haulier, transporting bottled gas was a great job, paying well and with no nights out. We subcontractors, were brought in when the weather became trying. A good season for us meant a cold winter, possibly lasting from November until late March. No initial training was ever given, common sense and assistance from more experienced drivers being the only education available.

At the beginning of my third season, a basic, theoretical course for the handling of propane was organized by the gas bottling company. Bolting horses and closed doors came to mind! All persons dealing with gas, either directly or indirectly were invited. Lads on the bottling plant, truck fitters, company drivers and an array of owner drivers and small haulers who had handled the products over the years were encouraged to attend the seminar. The course was to pre-empt the European introduction of paper qualifications. A situation was emerging where thousands of perfectly safe, competent drivers were staring dismissal in the face. Many drivers for one reason or another had failed to master writing at school and now faced exams.

A Saturday morning was chosen. All participants were welcomed into the canteen for tea or coffee. A long table, covered in snacks had been prepared for the break at mid-morning. The room was large and warm. Shafts of bright light streamed in through large curtained windows. At the appointed time we were asked to take a seat. A short, balding man with a monotonous voice commenced to give us the lecture. It proved to be an overall picture of future government regulations to be inflicted on the haulage industry. During a section on fire extinguishers and fire hazards relating to gas, my eyes began to close and my concentration waned. I awoke suddenly, with the elbow of my neighbouring driver being pushed into my ribs.

"You can't half snore," he said. Looking round the room, I could see grinning drivers staring in my direction, a number giving me the 'thumbs up' in jest.

"Have I been out long?" I enquired.

"Well you missed the food and the film. It's all over now. We left you there, you looked at peace!"

God knows how long I slept for but it didn't matter as I was now given my certificate of competence, meaning I was now qualified to do the job I had been doing for past three years. What a gift.

As the time rolled by, I achieved all the other necessary qualifications necessary for the carriage of hazardous goods either as package or by the tanker load.

The safety officer in Fawley was acutely aware of potential risks associated with petroleum and its by-products. All regular and visiting drivers were quizzed frequently on their knowledge of hazardous products and related procedures plus all safety equipment was regularly checked. The science of the stability or instability of loads was explored and actions to be taken were explained if a problem should arise on further courses held at Fawley. The company medical staff gave demonstrations on life saving with ''Anne', the plastic torso, being used for mouth to mouth resuscitation.   Choking was covered in depth and included a demonstration of the Heinnrik Manoeuver. Information and skills, learnt on these occasions, were useful in everyday life and became relevant within a few days of one of these courses.

Whilst driving through the lower part of Southampton I arrived at a busy set of traffic lights and had to halt. As I waited, a car driven by a woman and containing two young girls, pulled up on my right. One passenger wound down the window and the driver leant over to ask directions. Unfortunately the lights changed so I asked her to find a suitable stopping place. This she did and all three occupants subsequently piled out. Having pulled up behind their vehicle, I too got out and stood between the driver and one of the girls before commencing the arduous job of trying to explain simple directions to the woman driver. Please note this is not a characteristic of all women in general, just this prat.

A couple of minutes into the speech, a coughing and choking sound emanated from the girl at my side. I turned to see the young female, aged about fourteen, turning shades of blue and red. Her eyes were glazing over and she looked terrified holding her fingers to her throat. Without hesitation, I stood behind her, trying to remember the Heinrik Manoeuvre from a few days previously. Putting my arms around her chest I squeezed hard and fast. It worked! Within seconds, a sweet or lump of gum shot from her mouth like a stone from a catapult to bounce and skip across the carriageway. Thankfully, her face immediately returned its normal youthful colour. It is difficult to believe the speed at which she had become so close to death. When the driver turned to face me to continue our conversation, the girl had recovered. Her mother was obviously totally unaware of her daughter's horrifying experience as nothing was mentioned. Later at home I reiterated the story to my wife and she responded by saying," Yes love, what do you want for tea?"

I had just saved a life! A medal would have been nice-at least a little recognition for my heroism would have been wonderful; a sentence in the local press with a small mention of my heroics would have been satisfying, but no, it was just a question about food!

CHAPTER FIFTEEN

To Spain with Jim

In the early-eighties I was overcome with a desire to import Spanish slates, known as pizarra. The reason for this loony idea came about through circumstances when my wife and I purchased the property next door, the semi adjoining our dwelling. The reason for this investment was to provide an extra bedroom to our house for our youngest son. Having purloined the room from the new house, we had decided to convert the remainder of the building into flats for a long term investment. The roofs of both houses were in poor condition with valleys occurring where there should have been ridges; holes and leaks supplying a secondary source of water when it rained! A need for a complete rebuild was a top priority. My wife had secured a quote from a local roofing company which seemed excessive so a possible DIY project looked imminent.

I think it was at this point that the possibility of importing slates looked an attractive line of investigation and I remember spending many hours in the local library researching suppliers of natural slate. Armed with this information I sent off many letters of enquiry to quarries in northern Spain requesting samples of their product. The internet had yet to be invented; letters and telex were the only means of communicating internationally. The resultant replies gave me visions of making easy money. A short cut to early retirement, luxury cars and maybe my own farm with more pigs! There were very few importers of this 'old fashioned' commodity at the time. I had a chance to generate and exploit, what looked like, a vast, untapped market and I could not resist the challenge. My imagination ran amok and in due course I had invested in a fork lift, made a specialist brick crane trailer and spent hours 'cold selling' to building and roofing merchants. Fliers were dispatched to all parts of the U.K. Initially there was resistance to this 'old fashioned product' as concrete tiles were the 'in thing', retro was to be a feature of the future. I was a man of vision!

The first step in this enterprise was to obtain a large number of samples for BSI testing and for hawking around potential customers. I did my home-work from the small batches of slates sent to me, eliminating what I considered 'duff' products for the British market, some being very thin, others too thick. One example of a poor Spanish slate contained iron pyrites which shone sunlight like jewels but when wet turned to rust causing potential customer dissatisfaction. Others were curved, uneven or with a cross grain causing a fragile slate, easily broken when the roofer tried to punch holes for fitting.

Eventually we decided on a slate from a quarry near El Barco in northern Spain just a short distance from the Portuguese border, a journey of about thousand miles. The numbers of slates initially required for testing and giving as samples to perspective customers left the Spanish Post Office out of the contest for posting. A personal collection service deemed the answer and an excellent excuse for a day out in France and Spain. The prospect of my first visit to Spain I found exhilarating with the chance to see, for myself, orange groves and taste Sangria or Fundador.

Plans were put in motion, the excitement of the forth-coming journey being relayed in casual conversation to just about everybody in our yard. Jimmy, one of the Taylor brothers who were ferrous and non-ferrous recyclers of the realm showed great interest in my plans for the impending trip. The year previously he had been taken to the bright lights and one armed bandits of Las Vegas by his family. Further conversations exposed a lack of confidence in the undertaking of further world travel. The seed of exploration had been sown in America but the prospect of further globe-trotting opportunities for him had been limited. When the chance of a free trip to Spain arose, Jim took little persuasion.

I have always acted on impulse. "Why wait until next week?" so when he asked when the trip was to take place, I replied without hesitation, "How about tomorrow?" Who needs to book a hotel when they have a car in which to sleep? A thousand miles is about a full day's hard drive, give or a take a break or two. I telexed the quarry with our intentions of visiting them in a quest for samples and their instant response stated that we would be welcome at any time.

The idea of spending hours packing innumerable amounts of clothing for every eventuality has never appealed to me. When family holidays have occurred, my wife has done the case stuffing, checking off items from a list created after weeks of thought. As for me, a small sports bag containing the essentials sufficed. Local shops have always come to the rescue for forgotten items. My philosophy was echoed by Jim who was also a 'one bag man'. When participating in his daily tasks, he dressed the part of a scruffy working man and often wore black engine oil as unintentional makeup. However, when it called for more important activities, he scrubbed up well, in fact he positively glowed. Wearing a pristine white shirt with open collar and an expensive soft leather coat which any professional football player would have been proud to call his own, Jim threw his bag on to the rear seat of my car.

"Let's go Chris," he said excitedly.

Our journey was to Cherbourg via the ferry from Portsmouth, then to travel directly south, through Bordeaux to Irun and Spain. We would hook right to Oviedo and then take a sharp left to Leon and Ponferrada. Our destination was the small town of El Barco. I did not question our fifteen year old Volvo Estate's ability to handle the miles. These old dogs were as reliable as the inevitability of taxes. To be on the safe side, I always carried a full set of tools and spare fan belts, this ammunition was usually sufficient to keep bad luck at bay.

As we drove through Brittany conversation turned to our youth. Jim, a number of years older than me, was from a large family and had many close friends. Childhood was spent pursuing magical days in woods and fields interspersed with earning money from his father by splitting logs in the garden shed. His dad supplied all the army barracks on Salisbury Plain with kindling wood, a lucrative and regular job. The free spirit of his young life was developed from having a secure upbringing where love, trust and respect were the key ingredients. On his death a few years ago, I was honoured to be invited, by his family, to his funeral as a true and trusted friend. The simple service was attended by hundreds of mourners, a suitable farewell to a well-respected man.

Jim was an eight year old child when the Second World War was declared. At its conclusion in '45 he was a lanky youth with an abundance of knowledge on self-preservation. Jim to the world was a quiet man, very thoughtful and canny. What he lacked in school education he made up with business acumen. The war years were spent skipping school to run errands for American troops who would pay with stockings, chocolate and fags. All these commodities were scarce and found willing buyers among the young ladies of the area.

Making scouring pads from commercial wire wool, an abundant product, even during the austerity of the war, added to the family coffers. The cutting up and melting in the bath of bars of carbolic soap followed by the decanting of this precious liquor into old beer bottles produced disinfectant and cash. This concoction would adorn the kitchen of many a proud housewife. However, if the concentration was too high, dermatitis would be a problem! Jim's family background precluded him from mainstream commerce. He had boasted to me, that he could walk down any street in the land and make, by using his wits, the weekly wages of the average working man. Scrap, is like foreign currency, it only takes a middleman to turn it into currency.

Jim's year, when he was not dealing in metal was broken down into seasons. Christmas was wreath and tree time. His Bedford TK complete with greedy boards, brushed out and badly cleaned of oil traces, would travel to Scotland where negotiations with forest owners took place. There he prepared Christmas trees with a chain saw and 'elbow grease'. Nightly slumber followed a few bevies were taken in his cab. The parcel shelf usually kept for his dog became his cradle of choice, suffering a few cold nights in a cab was nothing when he could ensure, yet again, a joyous season of good will from his loyal band of customers built up through years of trading. Strawberries, picked at PYO farms, repacked into punnets and sold door to door, gave summer income while a trip to the New Forest provided a wealth of heather. These few stems, rolled up in Baco foil or old silver paper from cigarette packets, became instant lucky charms when sold from a wicker basket. "God Bless Yer," became a regular statement when pocketing a few quid from superstitious punters.

My upbringing was by nature in complete contrast. Jim was a student of life, able to play with mates while, from my point of view, my only brother and I were prisoners in an isolated cottage. As a child it was almost impossible to associate with the native kids as they lived miles away. Many times I would watch from the local bus the village children playing games in a disused sandpit. I have looked through brightly lit windows to see kids enjoying birthday parties, but they never took place in our house.

Due to galloping dyslexia, unrecognized in the fifties and sixties, my school reports always gave rise for concern with the resultant penalties at home. My class work, adorned on every other page with red ink with the repetitive statement of 'see me.' did little to boost my confidence. I have always tried my best but to no avail. The only respite from this stream of ruddy ink was wood work, my favourite subject, a time when I could use my hands and not brains.

Discipline here was easy, any lad speaking out of turn or trying to be funny, received an instant volley of wood off cuts about his person. At the age of fourteen I spent two terms ducking low flying timber to arduously manufacture a tea trolley which, when completed I had planned to proudly trundle home as a gift for my mother. In due course the great day arrived and with excited anticipation. I remember hoping for some degree of recognition, a compliment or some form of endearment for the effort I'd painstakingly put into its construction, I gave it to my mum. My wish for any thanks failed to transpire when told to take it too and leave it with the old woman next door. Obviously I had very little skills with either my hands or brains and the old dear must have possessed poor eye sight.

I spent years trying to prove I was not a disaster, but on hind sight it was a complete and utter waste of time. The quest for appreciation has stayed with me for most of my life and possibly accounts for my desire to prove myself successful, working long hours in an effort to achieve the goal.

As time progressed I became a bit of a loner, not a weirdo but a person who can enjoy his own company. When as a young child, shyness was always a problem, and even when an adult I have had difficulties answering the phone. Backing into corners of the school playground provided me with some kind of protection and so to have a job driving for days without company has never been a problem, in fact, the love of the open road and my own thoughts is now in my blood. Like corpuscles, I cannot live without them.

Jim's career skills had been learnt on the job with the support of his family whereas I gathered mine from Salisbury Art College, studying Industrial, Commercial and Fashion Photography for 3 years. On completion of the course I felt qualified to take on anything the photographic world could throw at me. If only life and events were that easy, there is never a straight course only twisting bends to send you down strange roads. Often bumpy often sad but over time usually funny, a butterfly flaps its wings in Brazil and the whole world can change. When I left college I had the choice of three jobs. First being a career with the BBC natural history unit in Bristol as a small cog in British broadcasting. Second was an opportunity in London as a 'dog's body' plus a pepper corn pay packet with the world famous fashion photographer, Parkinson. The alternative was to go to sea as a ship's photographer. Due to lack of financial support, I mistakenly chose the sea and a strange route to haulage! With hind sight I realise I should have worked in a pub or done anything extra to boost my income in order have the opportunity of working with the photographer, Parkinson.

Having secured a job as one of four photographers on the Reina Del Mar, a converted cargo ship, I spent a few trips cruising around the eastern Atlantic and the Mediterranean. The object of the employment was to photograph passengers, known as bloods, enjoying the functions aboard ship. The captain's cocktail evening was a good little earner. Edwardian dances where everyone made their own fancy clothes out of crepe paper and whatever else came to hand produced excellent returns. When passengers went ashore with Cook's Tours (that is Thomas Cook not the ships chef), we photographers were in close pursuit to catch the punters relaxing on shore excursions. Wine lodges on Madeira or mint tea in Fez produced one pissed and often sick photographer.

My next ship was the 'Pendennis Castle', a mail ship doing regular round trips to Durban, South Africa calling at Cape Town, Port Elizabeth and East London. I was now on my own, a photographer, film processor and in charge of marketing. I travelled as super numerary with the same status as the dancers and hair dressers. I was employed and over paid by an independent company with the added bonus of an extra five pence per week from Union Castle in order to be under the captain's orders. These extra coins never did make it to my pocket so in theory I am still owed about a quid. I travelled first class so meals were taken in the first class lounge, the haunt of film stars and the filthy rich. I had my very own steward who looked after my cabin and arranged all the cleaning of linen and clothes. In the tropics the changing of clobber was a paramount concern if the heat and high humidity with its resultant fragrances were to be kept under control. Four thirty every afternoon, when at sea, saw the arrival of a large tray of cakes to the steward's galley, a welcome break from the tedium of slow hot days and the chatting up of young females. I had regular warnings from the captain via one of the officers to spread my favours among the females equally and not to reserve them for one. A statement that still puzzles me!!!!!

A six week voyage involved about two weeks work, a dream job for many but not me. This lack of graft resulted in hours of boredom. A state of affairs which drove me to ship's bar and eventually to chucking in my notice. My employers were not amused as I was their biggest earner, their number one man, God knows what the other photographers did, possibly fiddled or procreated as there was ample time plus opportunity for both. A subsequent offer of a transfer to Shaw Seville's ship the 'Northern Star' as chief photographer was a position I could not refuse. This was to be a generously paid job sailing round the world but came with one small problem. A wait of three weeks was required before the ship made port, an opportunity to earn a few quid ashore which I relished. A short term job on a local farm to while away the days became a way of life that captured my time for four and a half years.

Working with pigs, extremely clever animals looked like a new career opportunity. Over time, the job gave way to half days enabling me to build up a small pig herd in partnership with my brother. He worked full time with a bank and could only help at weekends and evenings. It was during this part of my life I met and fell in love with my wife. One year, one month and a day after meeting I proposed badly but thankfully she agreed. Having decided to be wed, the pigs had to go as the income produced from this venture was not enough for the needs of a young couple. Yet again another new career path was sort. I tried welding using skills and knowledge learnt at college whilst farming. This was soon forsaken due to noise, boredom and the need to work indoors helping to produce a fork truck chassis. An HGV driving course ensued with a short stint driving a tipper while a post as fitter with the local bus company would eventually help with the rebuilding my own truck. During this unstable part of my working life I flitted in and out of photographic employment, including working in the studio where my mate Pete, the friend who accompanied me to Switzerland, worked.

I have since been informed that the Northern Star was so badly damaged in a South Atlantic storm that it was sent straight to a breakers yard in the Far East before the end of the world voyage.

To continue the story and as the day progressed, Jim and I found ourselves driving through the endless miles of flat fields across south west France. The monstrous lines of automatic watering systems, spread like eels across the fields and were a novelty to Jim. The vineyards of Bordeaux were a new visual sensation. As we approached Irun, at the end of a long day, tiredness descended on the pair of us like a thick fog. Finding a place to eat and sleep became a priority. The idea of finding a 'value for money' establishment was discarded, any priced hotel would do! A venue with a large car park was eventually found. This is the last and only memory I have of the place. On turning off the engine the pair of us fell into a deep sleep. I suppose the effort of getting out of the vehicle had been too great a job to entertain. We awoke to the early spring dawn, with its chilly air, diluted mists and low light. With hunger pains and cold cramped limbs we started our second day. It was decided, as it was so early, that we would leave France and enter Spain before entertaining the idea of finding food.

Within an hour we passed though the frontier at Irun and moved on into Basque country. The first signs of a different culture emerged. Red roof tiles, hung precariously from dirty white houses, wood and glass balconies were stacked like boxes above each other and the first of many iconic examples of old Spanish architecture. Everything looked worn or bleached. A good coat of paint would not go amiss.

Breakfast was eaten in a café come bar on the road to Bilbao. Neither, Jim nor I had any knowledge of Spanish except for 'please' and 'thank you'. Outside the chosen eatery were parked a good dozen heavy trucks, not in a layby or designated parking area, but just abandoned on the kerb, like discarded litter. If it was good enough for Spanish truck drivers it was good enough for us. As we entered the noisy place a hush descended like a thick duvet. This was the first time I have heard silence. All eyes were upon us and watched our every move as if we had walked in, un-invited, on a private conversation. Our white faces, our clothes had caused suspicion or even offence. We made our way to the glass serving counter below which was a selection of cheeses and bread. Flies could be seen circling within, probably cousins of the ones darting and circling around the ceiling. An old woman in a flowery dress and head scarf appeared from another room and spoke. We were clueless. I assumed she wanted to take an order. I was hoping for a traditional breakfast, whatever that was, but without a picture menu I could to do little but point to the cheese and bread in the cabinet below. A cup of tea would have been nice, but the vocabulary was missing along with the dictionary I had left at home. I pointed at the San Miguel.

"Der," I said and raised two fingers in a gesture to convey how many drinks. On hind sight, a better way of communicating could have been selected. This breakfast, unusual in content, was welcome.

Asturias, the northern part of Spain around Oviedo, was incredible. Its beauty was a well-kept Spanish secret, a place where the population of Madrid flocked in summer. It was a cool retreat to where people escaped from the searing heat of the capital. Brightly coloured fishing boats adorned the little harbours with quay sides festooned with nets and lobster pots. Rugged fishermen sat and repaired their fishing gear in the early morning sun. Rocky coves offered up cool Atlantic waters to visiting families. In the country, lush valleys trapped small farms. Old wooden buildings, crippled with age sat on wooden pillars. Last year's crops of onions and cobs of maize still hung in long clusters over twisted hand rails. Low cottages, of mud and flat stones were sprinkled, like confetti, along tree lined carriage ways.

On reaching Oviedo we easily found the road south to Leon and took the old mountain route to save the toll fee. I understood why this road was replaced with a modern highway. Our track weaved and followed the contours the mountain, twisting and gripping painfully to the edge, a shepherd's crook looked straighter than some of the bends. Sheer drops, with little evidence of safety barriers ensured driver concentration. Old ladies, heads shrouded in scarves, would occasionally be seen sitting on stone walls knitting and watching the passing traffic as if waiting for disaster. Looking across the valleys the battered remains of vehicles could be viewed wedged between rocks. Drivers got an eerie reminder of the consequences of inattentive driving! Snow, glistening in the morning light, could still be seen on distant mountain peaks even though it was now late spring.

Mid-afternoon found us approaching the out skirts of El Barco, our mission soon to be accomplished. Small farms, I think we would call them small holdings stood side by side on the approach road. The smell of newly cut grass filled the air. Wild flowers, rich in colour flowed to the highway edge. Fields of grape vines were showing the first green signs of growth following a long winter. El Barco looked an old town with a dash of modernization, a transformation paid for no doubt by the export of pizarra. New modern houses all roofed in slate, mingled in stark contrast with the old traditional buildings. Heavy dump trucks over loaded with boulders, trudged incessantly through the narrow streets. HGV's laden with pallets of fresh slate, headed out of town. Dust and exhaust fumes filled the air and blocked the nostrils. For some unknown reason the place instantly reminded me of an American Wild West frontier town of television fame. Maybe the raised wooden sidewalks lining some of the shop fronts had triggered my imagination. First job was to find a hotel, then wash and meet the slate supplier.

We checked in and were happily surprised by the perfect English uttered by the receptionist. The hotel was cool, marble floors and light painted panels surrounding the foyer giving an air of tranquillity. On entering my room, Spanish traditional wood work became apparent. Heavy, dark wooden wardrobes and cupboards gave a sombre feeling to the atmosphere. The large, high bed with timber headboard and a mattress that looked two foot thick, promised a good night's sleep. The view from the window was limited, dust and grime on the glass coming from the road traffic below and making outward visibility limited. I did hope the air-con worked! Jim and I had agreed earlier to meet in the reception area as soon as we had had a good shit and a shave. There is little to compare with the feeling of cleanliness after a long day's drive through the dusty heart land roads of Spain. When questioned, the receptionist pointed us in the direction of the quarry offices- it's so easy when you can understand the language.

The modern glass and stainless steel offices were quickly found. On presenting ourselves to the secretary and stating the reason for the visit, a pre-rehearsed scenario came into play. The girl made a quick phone call and from the next room a young well suited gentleman made an appearance. This was the quarry owner, who in turn, in 'pigeon' English, explained the itinerary for the rest of the day. Jim and I looked at each other in surprise. We had only come for a few slates and had not expected a royal reception. We were to be driven to the quarry via the town's co-operative wine bottling plant and then treated to a meal. A Land Rover was their choice of four by four, admittedly the Spanish assembled version. The young quarry owner admired all British quality cars, his favourite being the Jaguar. He tried to explain that a sports model had been on order for three months. I would be curious to know how such a vehicle would cope with the mountain conditions we were about to endure!

First stop was the bottling plant with a conducted tour by one of the operatives. Huge glass fibre tanks holding thousands of litres of wine greeted us on entering the structure. The guide tried his best to explain the workings of this establishment, but as he could only speak Spanish I think we possibly missed some vital points. The company secretary, who was accompanying us, did her best to be the interpreter. Seemingly all the local farmers supplied grapes in the autumn in exchange for bottled wine and a share of the profits. On exiting the building, both Jim and I were presented with two cases of wine each, one white and one red. A quick thought of importing this wine to England, flashed through my mind but luckily failed to stop, thank God!

Our itinerary continued with a drive up, what felt like, sheer cliffs and horrendous bends until the quarry was reached. Spanish quarries, or at least this one, did not resemble their Welsh counterparts. Welsh slates are cut straight from mountain cliffs, chunks of rock ready to be sawn and dressed. Spanish slates are excavated in huge blocks by the use of dozers from beds of clay and shale rock. Explosives reduced these spectacular lumps to manageable sizes for transportation in dump trucks to the processing sheds. Having been sawn into oblong blocks, gangs of local workers split and packed the slate for distribution into Europe by road or train. Our pizarra samples, the reason for our trip, were loaded into the Land Rover to be later transferred to our car.

On returning to town we were escorted to a restaurant above a barber's shop. It was explained that the meals there were traditional, made by the Spanish for their own consumption, none of your holiday food of the Costas to keep the tourists happy. Garbled, excited speech could be heard as we climbed the stairs. As we crossed the room to our selected table, men rose and shook the hand of the quarry owner who in turn introduced us to these strangers. He was obviously a well-respected and successful business man in the town. As we waited for the food to appear, the local wine made its presence known. Our host pointed through an open window to the vineyards clinging to the hill sides, his finger indicating where the grapes had been grown. In the distance, strung high between the valleys, were nets, to all intents and purposes, enormous fishing nets.

I shall remember, to my dying day, the smell of the starter. It was crayfish fried in garlic butter, a delicate aroma for my nose to enjoy. The latter was a fragrance that would return to me when visiting Europe in later years. The next course was bird, two small birds in fact, smaller than a pigeon and looked like a couple of black splodges on the plate. Jim inquired as to what he was about to receive. The young quarry owner proudly stated that they were black bird or sparrow and again pointed through the window. His finger directed to the nets high in the hills. "Catch them in mountain," he explained, seemingly proud of the slaughter. Jim instantly reared up. "I'm not eating that!."

"You've got to Jim, you'll insult our hosts," I quietly said.

"It's not right, I'm not eating it."

"Put it in your pocket," I whispered.

After a suitable interlude this manoeuvre was duly undertaken, soggy bird filling the pocket of his soft leather jacket. The evening closed with our hosts returning us to our hotel and transferring the slate samples and cases of wine to our car. This heavily loaded vehicle now gave the appearance of a speed boat, bonnet sticking up while the rear sunk low on the suspension.

In the morning we decided to go for it and reach Cherbourg in one hit, toilet, fuel and snacks being our only reasons for stopping. The route home was to be the quick way, motorways where possible. Modern roads cut into the mountains made short work of the drive back to Irun and the border crossing into France.

At the first service area in France we were overtaken and gestured to pull over by the French police. I cannot believe it was the Spanish as their jurisdiction must have ended at Irun. As we stopped these storm troopers pulled us from our vehicle.

"Out Out," one of them shouted, before grabbing and slamming us against the side of the car. Our legs were forced apart and arms spread-eagled on the roof. Machine gun barrels were pushed violently into our ribs.

"Oh shit!" I exclaimed, "Now what?"

I was flummoxed and somewhat frightened. We were only carrying slates and a few cases of wine. We hadn't even collected any fags, an undertaking meant to be accomplished closer to the port.

The rear door was opened, good job it wasn't locked or they might have had the lock shot off. One by one each slate was removed and propped against the kerb. The more slates that were removed the higher the rear of the car rose until it looked correctly balanced. At the end of the exercise the officers also looked bewildered. I still don't know what they hoped to find, we were just a couple of English men humping slates. This scene that must have seemed a little strange to a Spaniard but we were after all English what do you expect?

"You go," said one finally!

The buggers released us and got back into their vehicle to depart as quickly as they had arrived leaving us to repack the slates. There had not been a word of apology between them. A quick stop at a cash and carry to pick up fags in Cherbourg before boarding the ferry completed Jim's day.

Arriving in Portsmouth, customs and excise decided to have a good peek at our vehicle. One of us must have looked guilty or the sniffer dog on the ferry's car deck found our car stimulating.

"Do you lads have anything to declare?" An officer enquired, through my window.

I 'm not a person too drop anybody in the shit or squeal, so a carefully worded response was required.

"No Sir, not me."

The officer redirected the question to Jim.

"And you Sir, anything to declare?"

"No," Jim replied, "only a few fags."

"Can we have a look at the few then?" sarcastically replied the customs officer.

On removing the blanket covering the slates, about ten or so large cartons of cigarettes were revealed jammed into every bit of available space.

"Could Sir please accompany me?" requested the officer. Jim reluctantly grabbed his loot and proceeded to follow him to his office only to return ten minutes later devoid of fags! His cigarettes had been confiscated.

I told them," Her Maj. can smoke herself to death, for all I care," was his only comment.

Getting the samples tested was easy. A full BSI accreditation was, I hoped, the first step toward vast riches. The following few months were spent collecting possible customers and orders, including a few slates for our own roof. Stormy arguments were played out in the bank manager's office. I had negotiated orders but without finance I could not proceed. Their refusal for declining me the money was ridiculous. The importation of slate was not good for the balance of trade. To be honest, if somebody with cash had imported the product, nothing could have stopped the flow of pounds exiting the country. Eventually having changed banks, I got a loan secured against our house. The limited loan prevented me from rolling orders. I had to order and pay against guarantees and wait for shipment to be delivered before collection of payment. New orders could not be placed until the cash was back in the bank.

Growth was slow and frustrating. I was quoting for major developments by building companies involving tens of thousands of slates with potentially large profits. Many years later, having given up slates for reasons that will become apparent, I was asked by my original bank manager for a meeting in his penthouse suite. After quizzing me about my haulage business, he apologized for failing to allow me to expand my slate importation enterprise. A decision that prevented me from becoming a well healed man of leisure. Bollocks!

The first load of slate was collected from Spain by me with my trusty F88, now set up as a six wheeler. A forty foot trailer was hired for the initial trip. The lack of loads to Spain at the time of departure meant I had to travel to El Barco with an empty trailer, but due to the potential profits to be made from the venture that seemed irrelevant. I sailed from Plymouth to Santander with a whole day at sea, a time to relax and make plans. A day travelling along the coast road to Oviedo and then left to El Barco, reminded me of the first trip I had made with Jim but this time, in comfort, this time I had a bed!

Spanish truck drivers are held in very poor regard by their fellow countrymen. In Germany, a driver is a professional with the same status as an engineer or teacher. At the time, I considered myself a businessman and budding roofing merchant. The employees at the quarry just treated me as a foreign driver. I had to get in the queue, wait my turn, giving the Spanish priority. The toilet was a wall and the canteen was out of bounds, a typical day in the life of your average truck driver. As a potential buyer I was treated like royalty but when I became a common driver I was treated like crap, what's new?

The return trip to Santander was memorable due to the fear evoked by the mountain motorways. There was mile after mile of steep gradient which dropped through cloud banks and interspersed with tunnels. Although, when on these steep hills I was in first gear, the weight of the load could not be held back with any ease. I had a twin-axle trailer and tri-axle unit with ten braking drums in all. At a number of points during the decent, I could not see the rear of the trailer for thick white smoke billowing from the brakes like an erupting volcano. The tell-tail smell of burning brake shoes filled the cab and lingered all day.

Spanish trucks passed me as if out of control, the fitting of electric retarders must be a major factor in keeping road deaths down.

Over the next couple of years I built up a sizeable list of merchants and roofers who took my slates on a regular basis. I was handling over half a million a year and took advantage of the shipping service between Vigo and Southampton. I became a regular face in the docks after collecting load after load for distribution in the south of England. Sadly this enterprise collapsed for a number of reasons. Major players, through watching my success, moved in and cut the profit. It's called being competitive. One of my customers declared bankruptcy, which cost me a few thousand pounds, an amount that wiped out the profit for the year. The final straw came when a London based roofing merchant died at the hands of armed thugs. I had delivered a full load of slates to a yard in North East London when, the owner, working in his office late that night, was confronted by a team of bad boys. Having bolt cropped the gates of my customer's premises they proceeded to remove the slates. When disturbed, a sawn off shot gun was produced. The resultant gun fire, I am led to believe, rearranged his face. I felt that it was time to call the slate enterprise, a day!

El Barco.

Quarrying for slate in El Barco.

Slatecutting and packing shed.

Awaiting loading of slate.

Motorways are so much faster.

CHAPTER SIXTEEN

Starter Problems

My love affair with the Volvo truck came to a sad end after a fourteen year marriage. Poor girl, although willing to work she found it difficult to arouse herself in the mornings. The smoke from the engine would take a good half hour to clear and, as already mentioned earlier in this book, the fire brigade was called on a number of occasions by overzealous members of the public. Her engine, although sounding fine, had lost a considerable amount of power and needed a complete rebuild or change. The effort of pulling 38tons instead of her designed weight of 32tons made her struggle. This was not really surprising as the milometer read over two and a half million miles. I had driven her most of this distance on the same clutch, no doubt this was also due for renewal. On hind sight, and with personal regret, this classic vehicle should have been saved as an example of great, simple engineering and not sent to auction for possible destruction. She was last seen exiting the UK on the back of a low loader, heading for Europe and the possible burning gun.

At the time of auction I had reverted to being an owner driver. Mike Irons had taken redundancy and headed for green pastures in Warrington where his mother- in law was encamped. Irish Jon, with P45 in hand, had returned to the land of his birth and the promise of a small farm for the price of the house he owned in Southampton. From what I gather from hear say, the knowledge he had about farming could be written on the side of a match stick and there would still be room for the head.

A casual glance in the 'for sale' column of the Commercial Motor put me in contact with an agent acting on behalf of a finance company. A six month old snatch back, a Mercedes with very low mileage was on offer at a very nice price. It was an opportunity I could not afford to miss! Initially I worked this vehicle with a tipper trailer out of the Midlands, but after about two weeks managed to engage simultaneously, two gears of the EPS (Expensive Piece of Shit) gear box. The resultant carnage was put right, without quibble by Mr Benz over a period of two weeks. I used this time to look closer to home for other good paying work, very difficult as the best jobs had disappeared in the early eighties. Every time the government put up the maximum carrying weight for a goods vehicle, the industry was faced with a twenty per cent overcapacity. In order to keep work, many hauliers refused to charge the extra so the unit price of a ton of product dropped.

An owner driver friend had recently changed from container deliveries to lift tank work. This was operated by a Dutch company through an English agent in Felixstowe. With my truck based in Southampton, it would have been nice work if I could get it and I did. To the uninitiated lift tanks are lift on, lift off containers capable of holding four and a half thousand gallons of liquid. All the truck needed was a low pressure and a high volume compressor, to blow the contents of the tanks out. I also needed a HAZ CHEM certificate then, hopefully, the job was mine. With my experience of modifications, rebuilds and creative engineering, the fitting of this extra bit of kit was no problem even if it had to be remanufactured from three defunctunits! A three day training course gave me the qualification I required and as the agent initially supplied the trailer I was back in business.

Over the following years my driving career, whilst handling tanks, was littered with unfortunate incidents, some were my own fault and others were created by other parties. On one occasion I was loading hot wax out a refinery in Wales. The product was destined for delivery to a customer in Europe. Wax is one of many bi-products derived from the production of petroleum from crude oil and is only a liquid form when very hot. For many years tanker drivers have had to assume total responsibility for loading or unloading when on a customer's property. At some installations or tank farms a company representative would make a fleeting appearance to check all was well and have a chat, but it was down to the driver to carry out the job properly. Having parked under the loading arm, opened the lid of the tanker, I switched on the pump. I had been informed loading would be quick but the flow rate of over eighty thousand gallons an hour of the steaming liquid was unexpected. My tank held four and half thousand gallons a load time of under five minutes was scheduled. The timing of the 'off' switch had to coincide with the timing of the product reaching to the top of the tank.

I misjudged the event with the result that hundreds of gallons poured over the top and dropped to the ground to disappear down a drain. The material remaining clung to the tank and trailer, solidifying in a thick snow-white crust with hanging dribbles like icicles. The product in the drains set immediately while the rest ran down the road like spilled custard. I felt sick, stupid and helpless. I gazed at the mess, do I laugh or cry? A passing operative noticed the new white dress my truck was wearing and approached me. He was grinning from ear to ear, "Got it wrong then drive? He said, laughing. "You're not the first. Take your truck to the steam bay and we'll sort out the drains." I was relieved to say the least! The steam off was quick and I made my way to the weighbridge before exiting the plant as quickly as possible. Very little was said at the time but a large invoice promptly followed, asking for compensation for one blocked drain.

Three times I cheated death by the thickness of a coat of Dulux. The first time was whilst working on the farm. On disconnecting a fork lift attachment from the tractor, I pulled away only to have the whole attachment, probably weighing in the region of half a ton, fall over. The vertical mast descended behind my back slicing my shirt in two from collar to hem. The seat was completely destroyed when it finally came to rest. Another quarter of an inch closer and a groove would have been gouged through my skull and down my spine.

Before the arrival of our children, Chris and I would on occasions, take weekend breaks with the in-laws in Crewe. Sometimes we would take our car. This mode of transport was often a stressful experience for me, the father in-law being an ex-police driving instructor and later, a ministry driving test examiner who frequently insisted I drove on family outings. Secretly I must have been tested a dozen times.

When circumstances permitted it was possible to incorporate work with pleasure. Regular loads of steel for delivery into Liverpool on a Monday could be transported on the previous Friday with a weekend break taken in Crewe. I would tip on the Monday and pick my wife up on the way home. One particular week, on an extremely wet northern night, a slow moving fair wagon dragging three trailers nearly caused our demise. My AEC loaded with sixteen ton of steel beams, nasty stuff to hold still even on a dry day, progressed up the M5. Chris and I, both feeling tired and beaten at the end of a long day, were singing badly together in an effort to pass the time and stay awake. An expected hot evening meal with her parents dragged us like a magnet towards Crewe. Heavy spray from passing vehicles produced a thick mist. The head lights of my truck failed to penetrate more than seventy odd yards ahead. Even though my speed was reduced to a sensible level, progress had to be made. Near Stoke the badly illuminated rear of the fair wagon loomed large and close. Its speed was no faster than a crawl. I had little choice but to break hard. As I did so, I checked my mirror, only to see my trailer of steel by our side. A huge black monster steaming with fury, water swirling like a raging river issued from its deck. A jack knifing trailer keen to cause a disaster and mayhem was at the side of my cab. Instinctively I withdrew my foot from the brake and swung out into the centre carriageway the trailer returned instantly to its normal position behind the cab. Thankfully the manoeuvre failed to clout any other vehicles but did produce the need for the clean set of pants that had been packed for the weekend!

The last occasion when my life was in jeopardy was when transporting twenty tons of phenol in a tank container. This is one of the most hazardous chemicals to be carried on the roads without escort. The product, used in the manufacture of weed killer and an important constituent in many house hold medicines, is deadly on its own. A drop only the area of a fifty pence piece on the skin will kill within fifteen minutes if not treated with an antidote. One wet Sunday I had to collect the loaded tank from Dover to deliver into Erith early on the following Monday. All was going to plan until I arrived near the exit of the last service area on the A2. Emergency road repairs had closed all lanes of the carriageway in front of services leaving the hard shoulder the only thoroughfare. The rain was heavy, earth bound in sheets. The orange lights from the works vehicles and cones twinkled on the road surface in quite a romantic manner.

At two in the morning this type of closure was common and usually offered very little problem for through traffic. Vehicles exiting the services were funnelled straight onto the hard shoulder. As I approached the exit point a coach leaving the site, appeared to slow and let me past then changed its mind. For no obvious reason it accelerated onto the carriageway about fifty feet ahead of me. This meant that a thirty eight ton truck and trailer loaded with extremely hazardous chemicals was hurtling at about thirty miles an hour towards the rear of a coach sedately proceeding at five miles an hour. Looking at it another way I was about fifteen yards from a solid wall with an impact speed of twenty five miles an hour. I didn't realize how good my reaction times were. Unable to brake effectively I pulled the steering wheel hard to the right. Thankfully the truck did not roll but the wing mirror clipped the back corner of the coach and shattered. The cones complete with flashing lights took flight in all directions as I was propelled through the line. On passing the crowded coach the passengers all gazed out in bewilderment possibly awoken by the noise of my mirror crashing against the rear. I continued to hurl past and crashed back through the lineof cones only to stop on the hard shoulder just in front of the coach. For some reason I was not filled with rage, I felt calm but cross that this idiot driver had endangered so many lives. I remember calmly turning off my engine and walking back. As I approached the vehicle the door opened, the driver appeared frightened and did not utter a word. No doubt he was pondering on my next move. Would he be in for a screaming match or just a thumping?

Politely as if in normal conversation I said, "Good morning. I did not appreciate that drive. You nearly put us all on the front page of every newspaper in the country. If we had crashed the chemicals I'm carrying would have killed everyone aboard. Please drive carefully in future."

To this day I cannot understand why I remained so calm, why I did not flip after such a dangerous 'near miss'? On returning to my truck I continued my journey. Looking back through the undamaged mirror the coach remained stationary no doubt a much shaken driver was slowly recovering. He could still be there for all I know. My five minutes of fame had again eluded me, thankfully!

Late in the nineties the profit margins in tanker work began to collapse, the truck was aging, even after rebuilding the engine I was beginning to question the reasons for staying an owner driver. Niggling problems began to creep into everyday operations that over a few months grew into worries. Mercedes trucks or at least mine had an inherent problem that only came to light after years of work. The engine would usually stop on the same piston. When trying to restart the vehicle the starter motor would engage the ring in exactly the same place every time. Consequently the continual pounding of the starter motor, slowly but consistently, damaged one tooth on the ring. On the odd occasion the starter dog would ride up on top of the damaged tooth and thus put strain on the rear of the starter motor to the point that it would break the incorporated clutch. I got use to removing the failed part and repairing it at the side of the road. This was no problem on dry days but wet ones a nightmare. On one particular nasty week of bad weather near Christmas I pulled into the truck stop at Junction 29 of the M1. It was late, dark and I was completely knackered. A good meal, a well-earned pint in the bar watching the visiting dancer set me up for a good night's sleep.

Next morning I awoke to find my vehicle marooned in the centre of a six inch lake. Under normal circumstances this would have been of little importance, but when I hit the starter button I was met with a loud bang. The starter motor had failed again! I could not afford a garage recovery and a replacement unit would incur a bill of hundreds of pounds. Why commit myself to debt so close to Christmas when I was capable of repairing the damaged part for pence?

For a few months I had been carrying a set of overalls in case the need to crawl under the truck became an essential part of getting home. I have never seen the point of travelling with a full change of clothing so I had little choice but to strip off and wear just overalls. December in Derbyshire has always been cold and that day it was also destined to be wet. Having climbed out of the cab I crawled on my back under the vehicle, cold water surging down my collar and through the overall. The last thing I needed was a cold bath. The offending starter was hastily removed and rebuilt, a job I had perfected through experience. I was now blue with cold and with a chattering jaw and shaking hands as if inflicted with Parkinson Disease. Repairs completed I slithered back under my vehicle to finish the job. As I lay there, up to my navel in cold water but doing my best to refit the motor all strength in my arms seemed to evaporate or the starter gained weight anyway the whole thing crashed back onto my face. Eventually having checked I still had all my teeth, everything was bolted back, I collected my bundle of dry clothes and shivering with cold returned to the café. Luckily Junction 29 has hot showers which slowly helped to return the circulation to my frozen body. As I sat eating my breakfast I pondered the thought, what if it fails to start. Returning to my motor still marooned in the puddle like a cherry on a Danish pastry, I faced yet another predicament. I had failed to realize in my rush to use the shower I would have to succumb to wet feet in order to reach the cab. Scrounging a number of pallets from an adjacent trailer a path of wood was laid to my door. I would like to apologize, if belated, to that driver for not returning the pallets to where I found them. Sitting somewhat proudly in my seat I just prayed all would be well as another spell under the vehicle was questionable. On hitting the starter the engine broke into life. I vowed to drive straight home, park up and do no more work until a new starter ring had been fitted.

Christmas was spent manufacturing a mobile crane that could take the weight of the gearbox and travel along the chassis. The clutch assembly and starter ring was replaced and all preceded without any major problems. An appointment was made with Lucus's for a day between Christmas and the New Year to reseal and calibrate the tachograph. This would ensure a prompt return to work in the New Year. All seemed well, but not for long. On the day of the calibration I received a phone call from Lucus' saying their rolling road was defunct and would not be back in action until the New Year. A new date was set and in the mean time I chose to work my truck. I could not afford any more days away from work. Christmas, and the cost of parts had made a very large hole in a very poor bank balance. Work was imperative.

Two days into the New Year, a bright dry day, the ministry set up an inspection point in a layby on the A36 at Landford. I have yet to see them 'doing a pull' on a wet day. Everybody was there, the wheel tappers, the coppers, social security and customs and excise checking for red diesel and the obligatory burger van was on hand. I waited my turn for inspection, a procedure I had been through many times in my career and one which I hated as much as I hated the dentist. The boys in brown tapped and checked every conceivable part of the rig. All nuts got a knock from the toffee hammer, all bushes checked for wear. Having crawled under the tractor unit one of the inspectors emerged to inform me I had a seal missing on the gear box, a fact I was aware of. I explained the whole story from Junction 29 until that day. The inspector seemed very understanding and stated he considered no further action would follow.

CHAPTER SEVENTEEN

Reminiscing

On many occasions, whilst being an owner driver and haulier, I questioned the reasons or even my sanity for doing the job and why I had done it for so long. For half of the twenty three years I had enjoyed the career and managed to make a good standard of living even if at times it felt as if I was making three steps forward and four back. I endured the last half of my driving time which showed diminishing returns for the effort involved. Fuel price rises and government regulations dragged the fun from the job. The attitude of brother drivers changed from a fellowship of men who would help each other, to men being more inclined to look after number one. When I started driving most loads were sheeted and roped. Re-folding canvas sheets after unloading could be heavy work but usually there was some happy, helpful person to help. This was a difficult and weighty enough job on a beautiful, sunny day but on a wet, windy, cold winter's night it became a trial that would not be entertained today. Drivers these days are chasing the clock in order that the vehicle stays profitable, hounded by the traffic manager trying to maximise returns. Consequently, except when a compulsory break has to be taken, it's each to their own, a selfish attitude that modern pressures have placed on the industry. Young drivers are not aware of the camaraderie that once existed among drivers whose common enemies were weather, noisy vehicles and physical hard toil.

To experience a glorious spring morning with mellow mists and dazzling sun creeping over the horizon, was amazing, who could ask for more? Driving gave me an opportunity to see the seasons change and enjoy nature in general. Watching the buzzards circling and sparrow hawks diving into the centre reservations to secure a meal was a sight to behold. I must have journeyed through Cumbria a hundred times or more and never has the light been the same.

Time when travelling, especially on a motorway, was an abundant commodity, that could be spent reminiscing on what my wife and I had tried to achieve. We hoped that our efforts to make a happy home had been achieved. We had wanted to provide a secure place which would produce stable young citizens. Even though it may have lacked a good coat of paint, we wanted it to be a warm, welcoming haven for their return. We had strived to make it a place to recover and revive before facing the world again as they became independent.

Probably we were at odds with modern thinking but we felt an old fashioned, 'Swallows and Amazon' or even a 'Tom Sawyer' type of childhood would be the best. The children may, at times, have been sheltered from the onslaught of media hype, but using their imagination and playing traditional games we hoped would help them develop into self-assured young people. Camp fires were made for toasting bread and melting marsh mallows on sticks added to the fun. The three kids and dog spent many a night giggling and laughing in a makeshift wigwam of plastic sheeting and scaffolding until tiredness overwhelmed them. When time allowed I took them on trails, sometimes at night to the local park, a nine hundred acre common comprising of woodland, streams, lakes and playing fields. With torch in hand, they would watch nocturnal water creatures go about their business. When shone into the upper branches of trees the light would show birds, roosting. Owls would screech at each other in a menacing if not a frightening tone from one end of the park to the other. The natural world is a wondrous place, from the tadpole to the frog and from seed to flower. All new experiences for young eyes we hoped they would enjoy. Beth, our daughter thought Girl Guides a brilliant spare time diversion from school. Summer camps and hikes were found to be fun and challenging. Stomping though a rain sodden New Forest with her best friend, map and compass in hand was considered an incredible day out. Our garage became a workshop where young hands learnt to wield a hammer and use a saw safely. I still have the results of my oldest son's first endeavour, two bits of wood held together with one nail. Over the years projects evolved, a weather cock was made by my youngest son and a soap box cart was constructed by my eldest.

Holidays were infrequent, none of your Costas or even Butlins. One year the purchase of a sixty pound caravan and a pitch on the site of a Steam Rally put the family off homes on wheels for ever. When the first night fell, the bugs aboard came to life. It was a very short holiday that resulted in a small profit when the offending vehicle was scrapped! Years later we ventured onto water. The hire of a barge out of Ellsemere Port was probably the closest my wife and I came to divorce. The whole family including grandma set off with due trepidation from the waterside museum expecting a few days relaxation. Anticipated pub meals on the canal banks were to be my idea of heaven. Getting pissed and falling into a boat at night without the worry of drinking too much was perfect. The first night found us parked or even moored at the base of a stairway of locks, the height of which surpassed the adjacent buildings. On informing my wife, who gets nervous standing on a brick, of the impending climb words were spilt. I had the choice of going back or getting divorced. As I have previously mentioned I do not give up or give in, mediation ruled the day! The following morning she was blind folded and the locks conquered.

A birthday treat for my youngest son, a visit to Chester Zoo was to be followed by a surprise party on the boat. The family celebration complete with cake and assortment of teeth-rotting goodies was delayed by our temporary home slipping its moorings and drifting with a granny aboard completely unaware of the incident! This was an episode that worried my wife but gave great amusement to the kids who with a little ingenuity recaptured the vessel.

True friends, those who in the hours of need or despair still worry for you are as rare as rocking horse shit. Pete, my surrogate brother and his wife fall into this bracket and have, over the thirty years of friendship, stood firm. Their caring manner for our kids, as if they were their own, has been a source of security to our children and pleasure to us.

Looking back, I feel the time spent, talking, listening, supporting and consoling in times of problems has produced in a family of whom we are proud. My guilt about spending hours away from home I hope has, in some way, been vindicated by the contents of this book. The hours of encouragement we have thrust their way, we hope have bolstered their self-confidence in order that they will reach their full potential. Our children have proved to be honest, caring, socially responsible citizens who value the meaning of life, fairness, family, friends and money!

As they all know and have realised for themselves, the importance of a good education and our lack of finances have, in part, been due to our desire to provide them with the best opportunities we could. We know it has all been worthwhile. They must have understood that life without a few bob is not much fun and it has, hopefully, taught them the importance of being careful with cash so they may never have do such daft jobs as driving a truck for little reward.

CHAPTER EIGHTEEN

That's it. I give in

When I first started tank work with an agent based in Felixstowe. I hired one of their trailers, a necessary evil at the time but an expensive one. Owning my own equipment became a priority if expensive hire rates were to be avoided. Once again my ability for creative engineering came into play. I managed to find a cheap, damaged thirty five foot tri-axle trailer which I subsequently repaired and shortened. The twist locks were reset in order to provide perfect weight distribution on the axles and a chemical pump was added. The latter was a 'Heath Robinson' affair, being made up of parts from numerous sources including elements from a Morris Mini. It proved reliable over many years especially when the delivery of a highly glutinous product was required. The pumping of twenty tons of liquid Mars Bars could put a strain on any equipment!

In the few months following the fitting of a new starter ring to my Mercedes, life was pretty uneventful. My association with the Taylor Brothers had opened up opportunities over the years to purloin many interesting articles of scrap. These ranged from parts emanating from the dismantling of a Vulcan Bomber, which were later installed into my old F88, and the purchase of a 1938 Aveling Barford single cylinder diesel road roller. This old veteran became a rebuild project for many years.

Years previously with the help of my mate Pete, I had undertaken the difficult task of digging the roller out of the ground, having purchased her from Jim Taylor for her scrap value. The beast, which in my eyes was a beauty, had been recovered from the farm where she had died and been abandoned twenty years earlier. The weight had, over time, made the roller sink three feet into the ground. During a spare two weeks, with the aid of heavy duty jacks and large wooden blocks, we had raised the old girl to ground level. The borrowing of a low loader trailer from a friend saw her begin the long road to restoration. When inspecting the engine block I could clearly see a seized piston and smashed big ends, no wonder she had met her demise!

This rebuild project lasted at least fifteen years. The replacement of worn out parts proved a challenge. Research led me to discover a company in Workington that manufactured a strange and wonderful assortment of piston rings for all manner of installations from steam trains to road rollers. As luck would have it Workington was a regular delivery point for oil additives, a frequently carried product. As I placed the order I knew full well I could collect the parts personally at some point in the future. A few weeks slipped by before I was required back in the vicinity and the opportunity to collect the spares. Having delivered my load, the relevant industrial estate where my new parts could be collected was located, but I failed to find the specific unit. Following a frustrating drive around the unmarked roads I rang the ring supplying company for help.

"Hang on" replied the operator," I'll look out me window, see if can see yer. What yer driving?"

I explained.

"Yep, yer outside the back of us," he said. "Park up and I'll come ter yer."

At the time of the phone conversation I was dangerously close to a road junction. A quick check of my mirrors proved all was clear so I commenced a slow reverse to a safer position. Another glance in the mirror saw my supplier grasping a brown package and coming towards me. As he approached he seemed to be finding something very amusing. I stopped and removed myself from my cab. On inspecting the rear of my truck, I discovered I had a small blue Ford trapped by its bumper under my rear bumper. This was no laughing matter. The driver, a young lady who was still in her seat, was crying pitifully.

"I tried to stop," she sobbed. "I pulled on the hand brake, but nothing happened." My supplier, who had obviously seen the whole incident unfold, grasped the moment.

"Jump out love, I'll check the brakes."

She duly climbed out and still sobbing continued, "I've just passed my test, this is my dad's car, he'll kill me if it's damaged."

My supplier checked the car but could find little wrong and by pressing down on the bonnet we released the vehicle. Somebody suggested that she should have her brakes tested and checked by a garage for safety sake. Getting back in her vehicle she wiped her eyes and apologised for driving into me.

"No harm done," I replied.

To this day I feel guilty as the poor girl had actually stopped so close to the rear of my trailer that she had disappeared into my blind spot and during my slow reversing. I had backed into her, in fact she was stationary and I was moving!

Snatching my important brown package it was obviously time to return home to continue the restoration work on my roller.

I often wonder if the fitting of a reversing beeper could have prevented the encounter but I shall never know. It would have been easy enough to have fitted a warning system; a couple of wires from the tape cassette to a small speaker at the rear of the trailer could have been adequate. A pre-recorded message could have been inserted at the commencement of the backing manoeuvre with a polite few words such as, "This vehicle is reversing, this vehicle is reversing, this vehicle is reversing." There again a more appropriate message of, "Out the bloody way, can't you see this truck is fucking backing you blind cow. Out the bloody way, can't you see..........." or any other suitable greeting.

Late spring of that year saw me delivering oil additives to a lubrication plant just outside Leeds. This was a plant I had visited on frequent occasions and if all went well, the job could be completed just inside my driving day.

One of the major problems and expenses with trucks is the wearing out of tyres. These can prove dangerous too if they fall off the rim, puncture or just explode. Prior to this particular eventful day I had a new super single fitted to the near side of my trailer. This was a regular expenditure and necessary if only to keep the Old Bill at bay.

Within sight of my delivery point, the crest of a hill on the M18, my attention was distracted from the Jimmy Young radio show by a boom, a crack similar to shot gun fire. One look in the mirror showed a cloudy screen of dust and a rotating flapping wheel. Having stopped the truck, I discovered an exploded tyre lay wrecked on the rim. The rush of air had removed a mudguard along with its stay brackets. Searching the surrounding hedge-rows I found only a few hand sized piece of mudguard. Little chance of refitting this even if I could find the supports, the steel hydraulic oil feed pipes supplying the chemical pump at the rear of the trailer had been bent and twisted like a donkeys hind leg. This was to be the beginning of a bad day.

A phone call to ATS, the national tyre supplier, resulted in another wait, but in due course a new tyre was fitted and two hours later I continued my journey. The day progressed without incident until, on returning home, I reached Newbury. Before the bypass was constructed all traffic crawled through the town having been held up by numerous roundabouts and traffic lights. The first set was the ideal place to apprehend trucks. That day a young copper grinning from to ear like the preverbal Cheshire cat had positioned his Noddy bike in the centre lane of the three lane carriageway. As I approached, the lights changed forcing my vehicle to come to a halt parallel to his bike.

The smiling young bogie looked up, "You busy drive? He enquired. What sort of daft question was that I thought to myself? I was having a bad day and he didn't help. Momentarily the words fuck off wanker passed through my brain as all I wanted was my tea. No doubt his mother was proud of him.

"Why?" I replied gritting my teeth.

Still smiling he said. "It's such a nice day we decided to look at a few trucks. You know where the test station is?"

"Yes" I replied.

"I'll follow you then", he retorted positioning his helmet on his head.

As I entered the test station he disappeared possibly to find another victim. At least he knew I had not done a runner. Once parked up, the wheel tappers commenced their task and it was not long before finding the lack of a mudguard, made their day.

"Sorry drive," said one. "You have just won an immediate prohibition, your very own GV9."

This to the layman means the vehicle or in my case the trailer could not be moved on the public highway without being repaired or transported on a trailer to a work shop for fixing.

"You can see it's only just happened. The damage is fresh, it hasn't yet rusted," I protested, in fact the broken stay glistened in the sun like silver.

If the same situation had occurred ten or fifteen years earlier I would have been told to clear off and get it fixed. The way things are progressing it will not be long before the driver is put in the slammer and the offending vehicle instantly crushed.

"Ah, that's not all, the hand break is sticking," replied the official.

"If I fixed it now, can I go home"? I asked again gritting my teeth.

"Fix it and I'll see, he replied.

A few drops of oil from the dip stick and a good half hour adjusting the brake cable correctly, finally satisfied the ministry man. Eventually he agreed to a delayed prohibition notice and I could at least proceed home. The reason for that particular purge was the introduction of lap top computers for test station operatives. A new state of the art toy to be played with but it took another hour wait before he was confident enough to supply me with the get out of jail certificate.

A signature on my tachograph gave me a ticket home and possibly ended the longest day of my driving life.

Next morning was wet, grey and mournful the type of day for a funeral. Hours were spent replacing and making good the damage to my trailer before returning the rig to our local test station for the lifting of the prohibition. On returning home a buff envelope greeted me on the kitchen table. The contents informed me I had been fined six hundred pounds relating to the missing gear box seal from the previous January! That was it. Sod it! After twenty three years as a haulier I gave up and I gave in, beaten into submission by exhaustion, lack of money and regulations.

An instant decision was made to knock my transport career on the head. Amen.

Loading oil additive on tank farm.

Bollocks!!!

Printed in Great Britain
by Amazon

45616051R00078